How to profitably delight
your customers

How to profitably delight your customers

Hal Mather

THE INSTITUTE OF
**OPERATIONS
MANAGEMENT**

CRC Press

Boca Raton   Boston   New York   Washington, DC

WOODHEAD PUBLISHING LIMITED

Cambridge, England

Published by Woodhead Publishing Limited in association with the Institute of Operations Management

Woodhead Publishing Ltd
Abington Hall, Abington
Cambridge CB1 6AH, England

Published in North and South America by CRC Press LLC, 2000 Corporate Blvd, NW Boca Raton FL 33431, USA

First published 1999, Woodhead Publishing Ltd and CRC Press LLC
© Woodhead Publishing Ltd, 1999
The author has asserted his moral rights.

British Library Cataloguing in Publication Data
A catalogue record for this book is available from the British Library.

Library of Congress Cataloging in Publication Data
A catalog record for this book is available from the Library of Congress.

Woodhead Publishing ISBN 1 85573 381 1
CRC Press ISBN 0-8493-0567-5
CRC Press order number: WP0567

Cover design by The ColourStudio
Typeset by Best-set Typesetter Ltd., Hong Kong
Printed by TJ International, Cornwall, England

Contents

Preface

Customers – those demanding people and companies are today in the driver's seat. This was not true prior to 1980, when most industries were in a seller's market. Customer satisfaction was secondary to efficient operations when sellers were in control.

Today, the majority of industries are in a buyer's market. Huge increases in capacity worldwide have outstripped market demand. Serving customers well in this environment is the only sure way to survival and profitability. But few organizations know how to be successful externally. Their policies, procedures, measurements and reward systems are all focused on internal behavior. Most managers gained their experience in the seller's market prior to 1980, so continue to push for the efficiency improvements that got them promoted. Being excellent internally is of questionable value, and could even be harmful, in a buyer's market.

So what to do? Firstly, to realize the only reason you want to serve customers well is to make money. Your objective is a higher return on assets. The objective is *not* to delight customers. Secondly, simply satisfying customers is not enough, you need to exceed their expectations or, in my terms, delight them. The reason is to stand out from the crowd. Your customers paid to be satisfied. There is nothing remarkable about that. Delighting customers erects a barrier to competitors, so they will have a tough job stealing your delighted customers away, and you get the positive word of mouth promotion with other potential customers that is invaluable.

The book's focus

Many books and articles have been written about ways to make the manufacturing side of a manufacturer more flexible and more responsive. This book skims these concepts. Not as much, in fact very little, has been written about things that product designers must do to design products that can be easily and quickly customized to suit the latest customer needs. Even less has been written about sales and marketing and the changes they need to implement to help a company profitably delight customers. These omissions will be rectified by this book's core emphasis.

Terminology

There are several different ways of describing a company's financial success such as return on investment (ROI), return on capital employed (ROCE), return on net assets (RONA) and so on. To keep things simple, I have used return on assets (ROA). This is simply because I describe how various actions can change the asset base. It keeps the discussion clearer.

About the author

I have been working as a consultant, educator and professional speaker since 1973. For 20 years prior to that, I held a variety of positions in a variety of industries. As a consultant I have been exposed to lots of excellent ideas developed by excellent people in my client companies. Sitting on airplanes and in airports for long periods of time gave me the opportunity to read the latest books and magazines related to improving manufacturing companies' effectiveness. Speaking at conferences provided me a free ticket to hear the other speakers. It is from this extensive wealth of inputs that this book has been written.

The reason it has been written is to fill the large gap in material that challenges past ways of behavior in design engineering and sales and marketing. It is naive to blame the problems of manufacturers solely on the manufacturing people. No question, they share a good portion of the blame. But many of the changes brought on by the alphabet soup of techniques, such as total quality management (TQM) just in time (JIT), enterprise resource planning (ERP), etc, have made great progress on the manufacturing front. Many past beliefs have been shattered and replaced by much more potent ideas.

This is not true for the design engineering and sales and marketing departments. In many cases they are behaving about the same way as they have always done. It is time to focus the spotlight on these departments and challenge some beliefs. My hope is this book will go some way to doing just that.

Hal Mather

Acknowledgements

As stated in the Preface, the ideas and concepts explained in this book came from a myriad of sources. It would be hard to single out any one. The cliché about standing on the shoulders of giants applies just as much to me as anyone else.

I hope I have not plagiarized your pet concept or idea. It was not done wilfully – it was just part of my learning process.

Thanks to Patricia Morrison of Woodhead Publishing for her help with editing the book. And, as always, thanks go to my wife, Jean, for her typing and retyping of the manuscript.

1

Today's competitive edge: profitably delighting customers

Every company is looking for a competitive edge – something you have nobody else does. In the history of manufacturing, competitive edges have come and gone. A new idea or management philosophy creates advantage for its proponents for a period of time. But then, either all companies embrace the same ideas or philosophies or the environment changes, removing the value these things created.

Those companies that stay ahead and grow are those which exploit today's competitive edge but are quick to discard it when it is played out. They, then, take advantage of the replacement idea or philosophy, to continue their upward path to growth and steadily improving business results.

Yesterday's winners

A look back at history will reveal the creation and then dissipation of advantages. While we are doing this, I challenge all readers to check whether their focus, measurements and reward systems have kept pace with the changing competitive arena. Of even more importance is to challenge whether the focus, measurements and reward systems are motivating people to work on *tomorrow's* competitive edge. If you are mired in the past, you won't have a chance of taking advantage of the future.

Low cost raw materials

The first significant advantage for industrialists came from the availability of low cost raw materials. You could argue that the strength of the United States came from huge natural resources, beyond any found up to that point anywhere else in the world. Add some clever designers and mechanically proficient production people, typically off the farms, and two world wars to provide the impetus for manufacturing on a large scale, and suddenly you have a nation leading the world in industrial strength.

You could argue that before that, the United Kingdom had the same advantage, this time getting its low cost raw materials from its colonies, and using its huge Royal Navy to block other countries from obtaining the same advantage. But now the colonies have all become independent sovereign entities, selling their raw materials to any and all comers at similar prices. And the United States' raw materials are either played out, or equal or better have been found in other parts of the world.

Ask your purchasing people if they can buy raw materials and purchased items at significantly lower cost than your competitors. It's a rare company that can honestly answer yes.

Low labor costs

The next advantage came from low labor costs per dollar of sales. This originally came about through efficiency programs, linked at the beginning of the 20th century to Frederick Taylor and his scientific management theories. Industrial engineering, methods improvements, automation and incentive systems all worked together to drive labor out of products. More recently, companies have reduced their labor cost in products by going offshore to locate in low wage rate countries.

These programs have all been so successful that, today, in industrialized nations, direct labor averages about 7% of the sales value of a product. It will be hard to gain competitive advantage by squeezing the 7% down to 6.9! And for some companies it is less than 3%.

I challenged you earlier to question how well your focus, performance measurements and reward systems match today's and tomorrow's competitive characteristics. Far too many companies are still measuring the labor efficiency of each direct labor employee, reporting this daily, weekly and monthly to the supervisory ranks, all in the belief that reducing direct labor will make them more competitive.

Forward looking companies realize that this is playing with trivia – there are significantly more important things with which to concern management than 7% or less of sales value. And of equal importance is the realization that there is a conflict between efficiency, especially local efficiency of a person or work center, and other business values, such as quality, inventories and overhead costs.

The issue of offshore production to reduce costs of products imported back home is a little more complex. But it is obvious that if labor costs are only 7% of sales value, then the gains of going offshore are going to be partly or completely eaten up with freight costs, inventory costs, customs duties and the additional overheads to manage the offshore business.

Hans Schar, President of Swatch watches, states that when labor is less than 10% of the sales value of a product, that he can produce anywhere in the world and still make money. That is why he chooses to manufacture in Switzerland, a high labor cost market, but where the skills of the workforce and the technology available to him give him competitive advantage far in excess of a small reduction in 10% of his business costs. This will be discussed in more detail in Chapter 10. But as a tickler, let me suggest that the import and export of large amounts of manufactured goods will soon stop, to be replaced by the export and import of factories, producing in the marketplace those previously imported products, but now customized to suit the local markets.

Technology

One hundred years ago, superior technology, of both products and technology, could provide long-term competitive advantage. The recent communications revolution has destroyed this route to a competitive edge. If you develop a better product or process, someone else in the world has a 'me-too' or superior approach within months and is now competing with you head-to-head.

Patents cannot protect you against this erosion of technology's value, for the following reasons:

1   Many less developed countries do not recognize intellectual property rights. They think it is immoral to withhold good ideas from helping them raise the standard of living of their people. Hence pirating is legal in these countries. It is hard to stop such products being imported into your markets and competing with yours.

2   Your new product or process advance must be described in great detail to have a patent awarded. Freedom of information laws now make this data available to all your competitors. By changing a little piece of your technology, your competitors can often get around your patent, in this case legally.

3   Proving patent infringement is a very costly and long drawn out process. The infringing company can often garner a large part of the market before the claim is filed and certainly before it is finally settled. Damages awarded rarely compensate the patent filer for the lost market share and the lost profits that would have been gained if there had been no competition.

There has also been a shift in most customers' perceptions of the value of technology. 'Build a better mousetrap and they will beat a path to your doorstep', used to be a factual proverb. Today, availability when desired, speed of response, service and reliability are higher on customers' lists of desired characteristics. You'd better have the better mousetrap in stock or quickly deliverable otherwise customers disappear to buy something technically inferior but adequate and available.

Quality

During the 1980s, significant competitive advantage could be obtained through a quality strategy. Large differences in the quality of competing products existed, which were recognized and responded to by customers. Today, this is almost a level playing field. Qualities of most competing products are roughly the same. Just to be in the game today you must have product quality as a minimum close to all your competition. I am not saying that there is no more room to improve product quality. There is. But the huge differences that could be exploited in the market-place are gone. Minor differences are all that are possible now.

Sales and marketing

Clever programs developed to encourage customers to buy your products can give you a competitive edge. But you have to publicize your great ideas to the world so it will respond. Your competitors get the same information and can copy or improve on your ideas in no time, removing any advantage you gained.

As an example, look at my own pet peeve, the frequent flyer programs of the airlines. American Airlines starts a frequent flyer program. In three months all major domestic airlines have a frequent flyer program. Who gains? No one. What do the airlines have? All the incremental costs of administering an enormous program that gives them no advantage. It's one of the reasons the airlines continue to lose money, giving away seats free to people who would pay for them if there was no frequent flyer program. And now overseas airlines are introducing frequent flyer programs that will give them no competitive advantage. My guess is they are introducing these programs as a defensive measure against the US airlines flying overseas.

I'm not saying that there are no good sales and marketing programs, but they should be structured to give long-term competitive advantage. As a minimum they must give a short-term advantage that reaches the bottom line. Programs that give no advantage or, even worse, no advantage but incremental costs, should be blocked. This subject will be returned to in Chapter 8 where I discuss demand volatility. I will challenge all induced market-place dynamics against your financial results, the only criteria that have business sense.

Today's opportunity

So far I have told you where you cannot get an edge on the competition. What you want to know is where you *can* get an edge. Before I give you the answer, though, recognize that the answer has a limited life. As the previous section clearly showed, advantages come and go to be replaced by the next. This process will continue forever.

Today's open window of opportunity, which will also soon close, lies in profitably delighting your customers. There are huge differences today in competing companies' abilities to do this. Exploit these differences quickly and grab market share and profits. If you don't move fast, you will see your competitors steal your business.

Why the word 'delight'? Many articles are being written and speeches given touting customer satisfaction as the objective. Isn't this the goal, satisfying customers? The answer is a resounding 'No!' What is it that triggers you to tell your friends, neighbors, relatives, work colleagues and so on about a product or service you bought recently? The answer is, either you received more than you expected, so you are delighted, or less than you expected, so you are dissatisfied. If you received exactly what you expected, it is unlikely you will find this unusual enough to warrant conversation.

How often do people tell others about a bad purchase versus good? Survey answers to this question vary from 2 to 1 to 5 or more to 1. Why is this bias present? Because humans like to bitch. Just look at what sells newspapers – bad news not good news. And anger is a more dominant emotion and lasts longer than joy.

If you agree with this bias, what is the minimum you can afford to give customers? Satisfaction. And, if you agree that for every target you aim at there will be a range of performance around it, then you must aim above satisfaction, hence my word 'delight'. At the worst you only satisfy customers but most of the time they are delighted. The caveat, of course, is you must do this profitably, not by giving away the store.

Xerox's experience

Xerox has done some analysis of the difference in customer behavior between being satisfied or delighted. They say: 'We are six times more likely to get repeat business if a customer is delighted rather than simply satisfied'. So it is not a minor advantage that delight brings, it is huge.

Wal-Mart's rules

Wal-Mart was a six store discount chain in Arkansas in 1970. Today it is the world's largest discount chain. Sam Walton, founder of the company, wrote a book shortly before he died titled, *Sam Walton, Made in America, My Story*. In there he defined ten rules of success. Rule number eight states: 'Exceed your customers' expectations. If you do, they'll come back over and over. Give them what they want – and a little more'.

Wal-Mart's return on capital employed (ROCE) is twice that of its nearest competitor. It is growing at three times the rate. How's that for profitably delighting customers? I am not saying Wal-Mart's success is only because of rule eight, there are obviously lots of things they are doing well, but it is a clear contributor to its competitive edge and financial performance.

Are you moving your lips or your feet?

A survey of more than 100 managers from Fortune 500 companies was made by Rath & Strong, a management consulting firm. The survey suggests that customer service, today's business battle cry, is mostly a new bit of rhetoric that receives plenty of lip service but little more. They found that 87% of those responding believe that delivering value to customers is critical to the success of their companies. However, 70% stated that performance is driven more by internal operating measures than external customer measures.

Please review your measures of performance that are routinely used to influence or motivate performance. Are they external looking, based on customer reactions, or myopically looking backwards at the past? If the latter, initiate a performance measures improvement team that will develop ways of rating your external performance. Reward those employees who help you profitably delight customers.

Eight things customers want today

I would like you to reflect on your current personal buying habits, for your family and yourself, for both products and services, compared to 15 years ago. What do you look for or use as buying criteria? May I suggest the following, based on informal surveys I have taken:

1   Availability.
2   Selection.

3   Delivery lead times.
4   Quality.
5   Reliability.
6   Service.
7   Customer-friendliness.
8   Cost.

Availability

When you want it you want it – you are much less tolerant of delay, being quoted long lead times or being given a rain check. At one time, waiting weeks or months for furniture, wallpaper, carpeting and cars was normal. This is still true today for very special or unique products but most normal items are available when needed. Customers' willingness to go somewhere else or to choose an alternative to get products when they want them demands this high level of fill rate to be successful.

Wal-Mart's fill rate is unbelievably good, a combination of a fast response inventory replenishment system and excellent demand information. They also have a more stable demand than others which makes availability when needed much easier. We will get to this idea in Chapter 8.

Selection

You are probably looking for products that more closely fit your needs and your life style, and there certainly is more variety available now compared to 15 years ago. But this is a double-edged sword. Many customers are confused by the proliferation of products that seem to have minor differences among them. Sales personnel often are not trained to explain the differences and why a customer should choose this model over another. And the dominant or growing outlets for many products, such as Wal-Mart, Office Depot and Home Depot, focus on only the fast moving products. They 'cherry pick' each manufacturer's product line with return on lineal foot of display or square foot of warehouse space as the criteria. They are quick to drop products that don't meet their objectives and replace them with others.

Manufacturers have been slow to take the same tack. Few manage their portfolio of products to maximize their return on assets, whether this means extending or contracting the range. This whole issue of optimum offerings will be covered in a lot more detail in Chapters 6 and 7.

Delivery lead times

This is similar to availability. Long lead times for even custom made products are frowned upon today. Business gravitates to those companies which can respond faster than their competitors.

Quality

The whole issue of quality has permeated the psyche of consumers. Whereas 15 years ago you were satisfied with, or at least accepted poor fitting doors, defects that needed fixing and so on, today this is not tolerated. Many surveys, conducted by such magazines as *Consumer Reports* in America, *Which?* in the UK, or J. D. Powers, an American company routinely surveying customer reactions to automobile purchases, give consumers excellent information on the comparative quality of competing products. Japanese automobile companies used these surveys extensively in the late 1970s and early 1980s to find and develop a devastating competitive edge, a reputation for outstanding quality *vis-à-vis* American or European manufactured products.

As stated earlier, many of the differences in the quality of competing products have been reduced or eliminated over the past few years. Now the term quality applies to the total buying experience. It is the combination of many things, including those I have singled out in earlier, or will in later, sections, as well as product aesthetics, ease of use, clarity of directions and so on. This suggests there is still room to differentiate yourself from the competition if you embrace this total quality view, rather than just product quality. But this view needs a total company approach and a whole new set of measurements and reward criteria.

Reliability

Fixing faulty products is time-consuming, either in taking or sending them to the service outlet or scheduling a repair man to visit your home. And it can be expensive as technicians and mechanics increase their prices to stay even with or ahead of inflation.

Customers today expect products to work first time 'out-of-the-box', and to keep going with zero or minimal problems for their useful life. Extended and complete warranties are expected, so if anything does go wrong, it can be fixed at the manufacturer's expense, not the customer's.

Service

This definition of service means the total buying experience. Is the sales person knowledgeable and friendly? Is the sales literature clear and does it highlight differences between models? Does the sales person and literature help you make the right buying decision among all the choices available?

If you purchase by telephone, is the operator helpful and does he or she get you to the correct person on the first try? If they have an automatic answering machine, does it get you through the selection choices quickly and easily or are you left listening to useless messages, waiting for your selection to arrive?

When product qualities become similar it is these aspects of the buying experience that become the criteria for deciding who to buy from – what I suggested earlier as part of the total quality program.

Some companies, for example Xerox, go so far as to survey not only the users and managers of their equipment but also the accounts payable departments of their customers. They realize that errors in their invoicing, failure to provide key information the customer needs on the invoice, and hassles over minor disagreements in the billing provide differentiation that influences the buying decision.

Customer-friendliness

Is the product easy to use? Are the instructions in clear laypersons' terms or technical jargon? It is a regular joke that most people cannot program their VCRs to record a program. This is because the directions were probably translated poorly from another language and by a technician who assumes everyone knows what the various buttons and their labels mean.

If you change your mind, can you return the product for a no hassle replacement of an alternative or a full refund? Mail order catalogs are great examples of customer-friendly behavior. The Smithsonian museum in Washington, DC, puts out my favorite catalog in which they sell reproductions of many of their artifacts. I bought an enamel bracelet for my wife one Christmas from this catalog. Shortly after Christmas my wife dropped it on a tile floor, cracking the enamel badly. I called the catalog company hoping to find a way to repair it. I explained to the operator that my wife broke the bracelet, but there was no hesitation to refund my payments in full. Now that is customer-friendly. As a result, I have bought and will continue to buy from Smithsonian, so they will recoup the costs of their customer-friendly policy many times over.

Cost

This always shows up in my surveys but usually at the end. You are probably more value conscious today than 15 years ago. You are a better shopper, able to judge the various attributes of a product that you are quite willing to pay extra for compared to some other competing products.

Are your customers any different?

The preceding eight issues were raised relative to your personal and family buying decisions. Are the customers of your company any different? If you are a typical business, your customers are looking for the same as you are personally. How well are you and your employees focused on providing these attributes to your customers' buying experiences? And that nasty question again, how well is your measurement and reward system motivating your people to look objectively at your company's performance through your customers' eyes?

Do you think your customers would be impressed and motivated to buy your products if you told them you were operating at 98% performance to standard? How about 83% machine utilization? Over or under absorption of overheads? Variances to standard? It is ludicrous to think customers will be influenced by such internal measures. But in far too many companies they are the measures of success. Large numbers of people are rated on their ability to positively influence these criteria.

If you agree with my statement that the opportunity for a competitive edge will come from your ability to profitably delight your customers, then measurements are needed to push everyone to support this goal. These measures will not be found in the traditional financial system. They will have to be developed from scratch and used as the key driver of the business. The financial system must be relegated to its fiduciary responsibility, to shareholder information and for senior managers to evaluate the result of their management initiatives. It must be replaced in all other areas with the new measures to focus everyone on the company's external performance.

Profitably delighting the customer

Figure 1.1 shows that there are two views of your business, the producer's, that's you, and the customer's. You as the producer know the first bar, your total business costs. Both you and your customers know the second bar, what you charge for the product. Only customers know the third bar, the value the product delivers in their eyes.

Producer view   Customer view

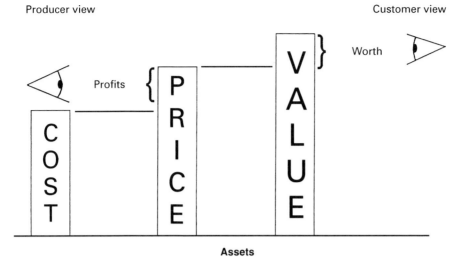

Fig. 1.1 Profitably delighting the customer.

The difference between the first and second bar is what you take to the bottom line as profits. It took a certain amount of assets to get this result so you can calculate your return on assets (ROA). If the second and third bars are equal, the customers are satisfied. They received what they paid for. The figure shows customers received, or their perception is they received more value than they paid. The difference I have labelled as 'worth'. They are delighted. If the third bar is lower than the second they are dissatisfied.

Earlier I talked about the tendency people have to focus on the negatives so that the minimum you can afford to give customers is satisfaction. It means you must aim above satisfaction and go for delight so that, most of the time, people will talk positively about your company and its product and reward you with increased orders. The trick is to do this profitably but, as you'll see later, it is no trick at all, just good common sense.

I mentioned ROA earlier. This is the ultimate measure, or one like it, of the success of a business. Return (profits) without knowing the investment necessary to get this return is pretty useless information. So the goal is to maximize ROA through delighting customers.

The assets portion of the equation is very important. Many times excess assets, caused by trying to delight customers, hurts your financial result. I will use the term, 'profitably delighting customers', rather than maximizing ROA as it rolls off the tongue more easily. Please ensure you realize I am talking about maximizing ROA, not just profits, with this label.

How to define value

The dictionary definition of value is 'a fair equivalent in money, goods or services'. It is when you get what you paid for. This could be written as the equation:

$$\text{Value} = \frac{\text{What you get}}{\text{What you paid}}$$

If the result is 1.0, you are satisfied. If greater than 1.0 you are delighted, less than 1.0 you are dissatisfied. This is not a very precise definition but at least it is a good starting point. Now you must know how customers rate your performance against this criteria.

Figure 1.2 is a bar chart with the vertical axis, value, and the horizontal one, various business attributes. Through a survey process of your cus-

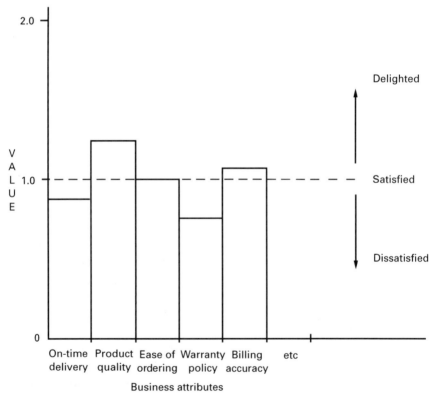

Fig. 1.2 Value defined.

tomers, plot feedback on their perception of your performance to each attribute. As you can see, some value ratings are greater, others equal to and some less than 1.0.

Which attributes should you pick? As a starting point, pick the eight attributes that typical customers want which were described earlier. Then reflect on the specifics of your business and add some issues unique to your operation. Lastly, be creative and think what your customer might value they haven't thought of yet. If you can be the first to supply them this, you can get an excellent jump on the competition.

This review of what customers want, but perhaps don't know yet, must be continuous. What delights a customer today becomes expectations tomorrow. You must keep searching for new things that add value to the relationship in the eyes of your customers and then provide these items cost effectively. This is the only way to stay ahead of the pack.

The bar chart you will create will now identify where you are falling down, so needs action. As a minimum, you want all bars equal to 1.0, with a few that customers are most impressed with greater than 1.0.

From sellers' to buyers' markets

Why has this opportunity to gain competitive advantage through an external business strategy occurred? The answer – because almost all industries have transitioned in the past 15 years from a sellers' to a buyers' market.

In a sellers' market, you pay lip service to customer problems or needs. You can be very profitable by focusing on the internal aspects of your business and optimizing them. In a buyers' market, the only thing that matters is customer perceptions of your performance. Internal performance is not unimportant but must be made secondary to your external performance.

The reason for this change is the recent huge increase of industrial capacity worldwide. Many less developed countries (LDCs) see industrialization as a way of employing their people and raising their standard of living. They also see exports of manufactured goods as a way of gaining hard currency to develop their infrastructures.

The recent growth of capacity exceeds the growth of market demand and this will be true for at least 10 years but more likely for 50 to 100 years. When capacity exceeds demand you are in a buyers' market as companies fight to keep their capacity fully operating. The winning companies and countries in this scenario are those which can favorably differentiate themselves in the eyes of customers.

A call to action

I will cover many ways to profitably delight your customers in the remainder of this book. I will challenge every business function to rethink their ways of behaving. Are your current methods structured to profitably delight customers or focused on a different objective?

I hope you will develop your action plan from these ideas to change your ways of doing business. And I am sure if you do, you will boost your return on assets, the only measure of long run success of any business.

2

Every company's mission

The goal of every company is to make money. More specifically, the objective is to earn a high return on assets. Manufacturing companies do this by transforming resources, such as equipment, people, money, facilities and materials into outputs of finished products which they sell profitably. These resources are configured or trained to perform certain processes to transform material inputs into finished products, which can be characterized as either for consumer, industrial or professional markets. The products are then sold into these different markets and into different areas of the world, either domestic or international.

The key emphasis should be on the speed with which the resources are transformed into products and sold to customers. Speed determines to a large extent if you will profitably delight customers. Of course, your selling price must be higher than your costs to provide enough differential to earn a profit. But most of the things customers value today come from excellent management of the speed of the transformation process.

Beware of the goal

A stated objective of one of my clients was: 'Use resources to serve markets better than competition'. What do you think about it? Is it good, fair, poor, excellent? My opinion is it is lousy. It doesn't relate at all to the goal of profitably delighting customers and the benchmark, the competition, is inadequate. I often tell attendees at seminars and conferences: 'Aren't you lucky your competitors are as screwed up as you are. If they weren't, you'd be in even more trouble than you are today'. Measuring yourself against somebody else's poor performance is not the way to improve. It is even dangerous.

Figure 2.1 shows two companies today, A and B. The performance being compared could be return on assets, quality, technology, market share,

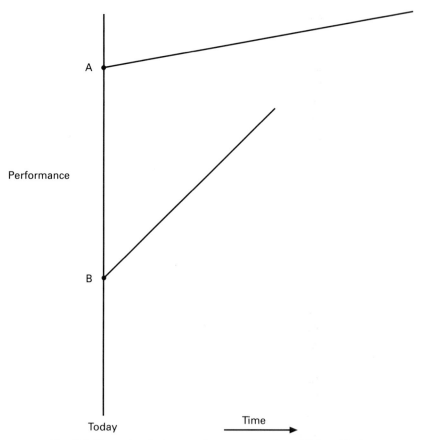

Fig. 2.1 The rate of change of companies A and B is critical.

management strengths and so on. As you can see, today, the A company is way ahead of the B company, so B is in trouble.

If company A used the objective stated earlier, complacency would set in, causing their rate of performance improvement to be as shown by their slowly improving line. Meanwhile, company B is improving their performance fast, as shown by the steeply sloping line. Now who is in trouble? The answer, of course, is company A.

There are many examples of companies in the A position being bypassed by others and hence relegated to second class performance. IBM and General Motors come to mind. They were at the pinnacle of their industry but their complacency allowed more nimble and hungrier competitors to pass them by. What this means is the position at a point in time is of passing interest. The position is bound to change. The critically important factor that companies must consider at all times is the fastest rate of change.

It is the slope of the line that is critical. This is true for both the A and B companies. If the A company does not have the fastest rate of change it won't be the A company for long.

What should a company change? The answer is, those things that will profitably delight their customers. This suggests a level of knowledge of customer desires and values that few companies have. You must establish a routine to reach out to the external market to discover what things customers want and to fulfill their requirements first and fast as described in Chapter 1.

Drive towards Utopia

How do you get the fastest rate of change? By comparing the performance of your critical variables against Utopia. I realize Utopia is perfection, so this is an impossible goal for most variables. But, if you ask yourself: 'How am I doing against Utopia?', and you find yourself a long way away, the only questions now are: 'How close to perfection can I get and how fast can I get there?' You are immediately thinking about improving the rate of change.

Use this technique in routine problem solving. First, define the Utopian solution. Now consider the problem against the realities which exist. You will be amazed at how much better your solutions will be than just starting to solve the problem without defining Utopia first. This technique is a great mind opener to the possibilities and the end result you would like to get close to. Thomas Watson, Senior, the father of IBM, said it very well: 'It is better to shoot at perfection and miss than shoot at imperfection and hit it'.

I am going to ask you several times in this book: 'What would you *like* a certain characteristic to be?' Before you jump to an answer, reflect on what the Utopian answer would be. This is what you would *like* it to be. Maybe you can't get there today but fast movement towards this goal will get you close.

Breakthrough thinking

Having the fastest rate of change throws into question some of our tried and true management techniques. Management by objectives (MBO) is a common way of setting goals, measuring individuals against these goals and then rewarding with pay increases those who meet or exceed the goals. The idea is for each person to set their own goals or to agree to imposed goals so that there is consistency across all levels of management and buy-in from individual employees. As soon as pay enters the picture, the emphasis thoughout the organization is placed on goals which are known to be achievable. Few people accept the risk of setting extreme objectives. This guarantees a slow rate of change, like company A in the example.

Another approach is to set what appear today to be unachievable goals – such things as double the inventory turns in 12 months, reduce scrap and rework 95% in 6 months and cut the manufacturing cycle time by 75% in 9 months. What these stretch goals are designed to do is change behavior. Success is achieving a good percentage, say 80%, of a stretch goal. This will get you a much faster rate of change than achieving 100% of an achievable goal. But this has clear implications for the way we measure and reward performance throughout industry.

Continuous improvement is not good enough!

Kaizen or continuous improvement is a technique suggested to get you ahead of the competition. The idea is to make small improvements every day so that, at the end of a period, say a year, you have introduced significant change. This process is excellent but not sufficient. Continuously improving today's process won't get you ahead quickly. You need break-throughs every now and then to lift you to a new plateau. Now continuously improve this new position until you can generate the next breakthrough.

The line for company B in Fig. 2.1 is straight. In fact it is a step function as shown in Fig. 2.2. Continuously improve the current situation until you can create the next breakthrough. Then continuously improve the new situation but keep pushing for the next breakthrough. Comparing your performance against Utopia will help you get the breakthroughs you need to have the fastest rate of change.

A study by psychologist G. Clotaire Rapaille found the following: 'Unlike Japanese workers, Americans aren't interested in making small step-by-step improvements. . . . They want to achieve the breakthrough, the impossible dream. The way to motivate them: Ask for the big leap, rather than for tiny steps'. Armstrong World Industries uses this philosophy to great advantage. They set stretch goals on a regular schedule and work to achieve them. This forces changes in thinking and behavior that pushes them to a higher plateau that they continuously improve until the next leap upward.

Most breakthroughs come from outside an industry

Look at the major and minor advances in products and you will find most of these advances come from outside the industry where the advance occurred. This is because of various blockers to change:

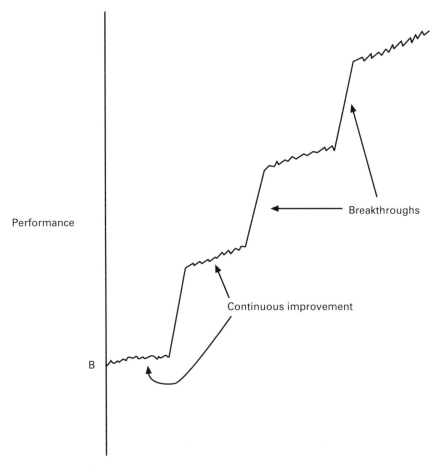

Fig. 2.2 Fast improvement is a step function.

1   You can't see the forest for the trees syndrome.
2   We are the experts. We know that idea won't work in our business.
3   We have done it this way for 25 years, what do you mean we have to change?

There is huge inertia to change and stiff resistance to dramatically new approaches in most companies. This is why breakthroughs often come from outside an industry.

    The watch industry is a classic example. The Swiss knew about the microchip technology but in their infinite wisdom decided customers would prefer the traditional jewelled movement. Along with this, their method of production, with many small component manufacturers feeding assembly operations, was not easily changed to the mass production techniques needed by the microchip technology. Texas Instruments developed their plastic watch, followed quickly by many Far Eastern manufacturers. In a few short years, instead of Switzerland being the major producer of watches it was Hong Kong! The Swiss haven't recovered their market share yet, nor will they probably ever, even though they have now embraced the microchip technology.

Utopia and stretch targets force radically different thinking *inside* an industry. You must develop the breakthroughs yourself rather than being blindsided by a stranger to your industry. You can get a large jump ahead of your competitors with this strategy.

Effective or efficient?

I described a manufacturer's mission earlier in terms of resources, products and markets. Another way of stating this mission is: 'To buy the right materials at the right time, process them effectively and deliver quality products to customers when needed. In other words, get it in, get it through, get it out'.

The key word to focus on is 'effectively'. I could have chosen, and would have several years ago, 'process them efficiently'. Assume you are the consultant now, not me. Go to a manufacturing company to assess how effectively they are operating by finding indicators or measures that quantify their effectiveness.

Let me suggest you would ask for details of the following:

1 Warranty claims.
2 Customer delivery performance. Line fill rate for a make-to-stock company, on-time delivery if it is make-to-order.
3 Internal levels of scrap and rework.
4 Inventory obsolescence.
5 Speed of delivery – shortness of customer lead time.
6 Speed of new product introductions – are they quick-to-market?
7 Flexibility to respond to mix and volume changes in the market-place demand.
8 Total inventory levels – inventory turns.

These eight items, plus others you may have thought of, give a fairly accurate picture of this company's effectiveness.

What if you again went to a manufacturer but now you want indicators or measures that quantify their efficiency? Let me suggest you would ask for details of the following:

1   Direct labor performance against standard.
2   Manufacturing variances.
3   Machine utilization.
4   Absorption of overheads.
5   Purchase price variance.

Now, the $64,000 question. Which do you think this manufacturer would rather be, 100% effective, but only 90% efficient or 100% efficient, but only 90% effective? My guess is you would say the former. This company would be much more successful with outstanding performance in the effective measures and so-so performance with efficiency, rather than the reverse.

But now back to performance measures. Are your performance measures, starting at the general manager and working their way down the organization to the shop floor workers and clerical staff, measuring, rewarding and focusing on the *effectiveness* of the operation or the *efficiency*? For the majority of companies the answer will be the efficiency, but this is ridiculous. 'People do what you inspect not what you expect.' You can't want effectiveness but measure and reward efficiency.

Please reflect on your measures. Start a program to convert your emphasis from efficiency to effectiveness. You will quickly find that most of the effectiveness measures are external – what your customer thinks of you. This dovetails nicely with your objective to profitably delight your customers.

Manufacturers' changing values

The move from a sellers' market to a buyers' market has placed emphasis on different values. These are shown in Fig. 2.3. The left-hand list shows the old parameters. They value internal excellence of a business but have no regard for external performance. In a sellers' market you can be very successful by driving these parameters hard. The right-hand list shows the new parameters. They value the external performance of a business, with no regard for internal performance. In a buyers' market you can be very successful by driving these parameters hard, as long as the internal performance is reasonable.

As mentioned earlier, effectiveness measures are largely external measures. Efficiency is 100% an internal issue. You can see immediately then

Old	New
(Internal focus)	(External focus)
Efficiency	Quality
Absorption	Value
Utilization	Delivery time
Variances	Flexibility
Standard costs	Total costs

Fig. 2.3 Manufacturers' changing values.

that in today's environment, effectiveness comes before efficiency. These terms have been defined as: 'Effectiveness is doing the right things. Efficiency is doing things right.' It is obvious you only want to do the right things right, not the wrong things right. Obsolete inventory is a classic example of doing the wrong things right. We made it very efficiently. We bought the materials to make the obsolete inventory below standard so we had a favorable purchase price variance. It is the lowest cost obsolete inventory you ever saw! But it is *still* obsolete so becomes a negative hit on the business.

Quality: external or internal value?

In Fig. 2.3, quality is shown on the right-hand side, meaning external value. But for the majority of companies, it should be shown on the left. This is because they measure their quality improvements through lower scrap and rework. But quality is not the absence of something in management's eyes (scrap, rework) but the presence of something in the customers' eyes. This suggests an external reaching out to customers to learn about their perception of a company's quality rather than myopically looking internally.

On time shipments – to our date or theirs?

Similarly, many companies which make-to-order measure their customer service based on whether they ship on time. But for most, the date they measure this performance against is *their* promise date, not the customer's request or need date. Is it clear that delivering 100% on time to your promise is *not* good customer service unless your promise date exactly coincides with the customer request. This is myopia again, focusing on internal performance to targets, not on external performance to the customer. Delivering 100% on time to a date that does not match the customer's need is lousy customer service.

Go with the flow

All business processes need to be evaluated against the objective of profitably delighting customers. The best way I have found to do this is to study the flow of product from vendor to customer and the flow of information from product design and sales and marketing back through the business and out to vendors. Managing these two flows well influences so many of today's customer needs. Delivery on time to the customer's date, availability when required, speed of response to the market-place dynamics and so on are obvious benefits. What may not be so clear is that obsolescence, quality, scrap, rework and costs are also improved with a focus on the flow of product and information. *In summary, improve the flow to be more effective.* Realize that improving efficiency usually hurts the flow, dropping your effectiveness when it is the very thing you want to improve.

This conflict between effectiveness and efficiency is one of the major hurdles many companies must pass. If you hang on to the old success strategies of focusing on your internal performance you can't be successful in today's buyers' market. Because there are conflicts, letting go of a little efficiency to gain a lot of effectiveness is the sure route to success.

The liquids analogy

I suggested that you study and improve the flow of product and information to become more effective. When you do this you will find most products and information do not flow – they lurch through the organization. They are worked on intensively for a few minutes and then sit idle, waiting for the next burst of activity.

Figures 2.4 and 2.5 show what flowing products really means. The market-place is shown on the right as an amoeba shape, inferring it is dynamic, constantly in motion. The company is shown as a rectangle, inferring it inherently is not as flexible as the marketplace is dynamic. This is because of the usual lead times to adjust production, such as hiring or firing people, buying new equipment, selecting new supply sources, changing schedules, etc.

If the company is not as flexible as the market-place then one of two bad things are possible. Make-to-stock companies can decouple the dynamics of the market-place from the inflexibility of the factory with finished goods inventory. Additional assets are hence created that enter the ROA equation, perhaps hurting it badly, or you increase prices to compensate, perhaps hurting your competitiveness in the market-place. And the assumption is that you can predict the right amount of the right products needed

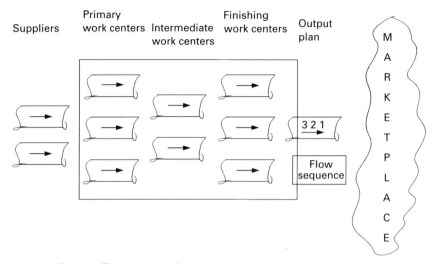

Fig. 2.4 The balanced flow.

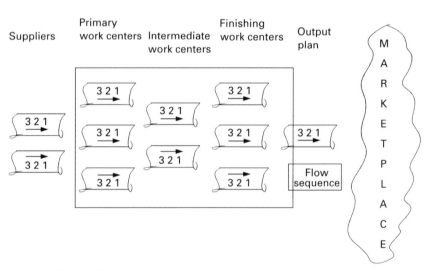

Fig. 2.5 The synchronized sequence.

in inventory to perform the decoupling activity. As most of you know, this assumption is dead wrong. Obsolete and slow moving inventory at the same time as you have back orders is often the norm. This becomes more likely the higher the market-place dynamics are relative to the factory flexibility. Forecast error gets you to make the wrong products so no or little decoupling actually occurs.

Make-to-order companies can decouple dynamics from inflexibility by quoting different lead times. When business is good, quote longer lead times, when bad, shorten them. But delivering to *your* promise date, as stated earlier, is not good customer service and certainly won't delight customers. It only guarantees lost business and dissatisfied customers looking for another source and hurting your ability to make profits.

Increase flexibility or dampen dynamics?

Two choices could avoid the negatives of the prior two 'solutions'. One is to increase the flexibility of the company to accommodate the dynamics of the market-place. The other is to dampen the market-place dynamics to fit the company's flexibility.

We will focus first in the early chapters of this book on increasing the company's flexibility. But it is obvious flexibility cannot be made infinite. Increasing it above a certain point will also be prohibitively expensive. So before you go and spend a lot of money and time on this exercise I suggest you read Chapter 8. The marriage of these two ideas, increasing company flexibility at the same time as you dampen market-place dynamics, is the best approach.

Balance the flow

Inside the rectangle on Fig. 2.4 are a series of pipes. This is the essence of the liquids analogy, conceptualizing that every business can be thought of as processing liquids through pipes.

Start at the right-hand side with the pipe labelled 'Output plan'. This is the output necessary to serve the market-place. This output plan can be broken down into two sections: first, the overall flow rate, as expressed by dollars per month, tons per week, units per day, etc, second, the specific sequence of end products we want to flow down the pipe and when. Obviously the overall flow is to serve the market-place in total. The sequence is to serve individual customers within the market-place with the specific products they want on the specific dates they want them.

We will focus on the overall flow first. The pipes to the left of the output plan represent a variety of machines, work centers, processing lines and vendors. It is obvious you would like all these pipes to be flowing at exactly balanced rates, balanced relative to each other and to the output flow in total. This does not mean that the capacities of all machines, work centers, etc, are balanced, far from it. It does mean that the flow rates through these machines are balanced.

Synchronize the sequence

Once the flow rates are balanced, the production of specific items or delivery of specific raw materials must be synchronized to the output plan. Figure 2.5 shows this clearly, the numbers 3, 2, 1, suggesting specific things moving down these pipes, synchronized to each other and to the output plan.

The Utopian business

What could you tell me about a company where the flow rate and sequence of flow from the suppliers is perfectly balanced and synchronized to the flow rate and sequence in the primary work centers; their flow rates and sequence are perfectly balanced and synchronized to the flow rate and sequence in the intermediate work centers; their flow rate and sequence are perfectly balanced and synchronized to the flow rate and sequence in the last work centers; with the flow rate and sequence in the last work centers perfectly balanced and synchronized to the output plan we know is necessary to profitably delight all our customers? I hope you say: 'That would be Utopia'. Of course you are correct as long as the flow rates can be quickly rebalanced if the market-place demand in total varies, and the sequences can be quickly resynchronized if the market-place sequence changes.

Seven benefits from the Utopian 'liquids' plant

The benefits of such a scenario are as follows:

1   Low inventories – the amount of inventory in this business will be very small, controlled by the actual value-adding portion of the process. This is minutes for most products, hours for a few and days for even fewer. Inventory turns of three digits annually will be routine in this operation.
2   Customer satisfaction – all customers will get exactly what they want exactly when they want it.
3   Perfect quality – guaranteed quality in this scenario is a necessity. Bad quality shuts this operation down. There is no tolerance for unexpected disturbances such as quality problems.
4   Short throughput times – the throughput time will be a function of the value-added processing time, again minutes or hours for most.
5   Flexibility – the short throughput times give automatic flexibility to sequence changes in the market-place, so that any product can be made in minutes or hours. Flexibility to make volume changes will only be

possible with excess capacity that can be turned on or off quickly. You see here a conflict between internal efficiency measures, such as high machine utilization, and external performance, responding to all customers quickly. High machine utilization guarantees inflexibility.

6 Low costs – it may not be immediately obvious, but most controllable costs today are the non value added waste (NVAW) that all companies have. The Utopian business would have low NVAW hence low cost. I'll discuss the NVAW concept later in this chapter and identify some key sources of these excess costs.

7 'Productive'. resources – you can tell by the quotation marks that this is not your traditional way of thinking about productivity, which is simply output divided by input. My definition of a 'productive' operation: 'resources are only *truly* productive when they are making exactly the right amount of exactly the right things your customers need right now' may not be seen as productive or efficient under the traditional definition. Anything else they make will absorb the overheads, give you higher machine utilization and keep people busy but, in fact, these are terrible wastes of valuable productive resources.

Develop 'liquid' suppliers

The obstacle to achieving all these objectives could be suppliers. We could be doing everything perfectly internally but slow, unresponsive suppliers would stop us achieving many benefits. So what would you like your suppliers to look like? Exactly like the liquids analogy shown in Fig. 2.5, of course. Your suppliers and you would share in the seven benefits of the liquids factory and your suppliers would behave like an integral part of your business. (Chapter 9 talks about all phases of partnering and the ultimate reason for entering these arrangements – high profits for both parties.)

It is your responsibility to select and work with suppliers to make them liquid. Many of my clients sponsor joint seminars, both with their suppliers and their customers, to foster discussion and agreement to the 'liquid' objective. They use these seminars as the springboard to partnering programs. Clear agreement on objectives followed by joint action plans puts them on the road to win/win relationships.

Liquids analogy/just in time/world class manufacturing

A lot has been written about just in time (JIT) and world class manufacturing (WCM). It is difficult to visualize an operation from all this verbiage. The liquids analogy encapsulates ideas from JIT and WCM, as well as some from total quality management (TQM). It gives you a visual picture of these concepts, but it goes beyond all these ideas suggesting a much broader scope. The design of products, the variety of end products, the dynamics of the marketplace and so on all need to be challenged using the liquids picture.

Figure 2.6 shows this concept clearly. If we truly believe we have to profitably delight customers to be successful, then all departments must be focused on the company's external behavior. All internal activities must be challenged against the criteria, do these improve our external performance or are they internally focused?

Some of the challenges that will be discussed in later chapters are shown in each department's 'pipe'. Getting parallel improvement programs going in every department is the path to dramatic change and benefits.

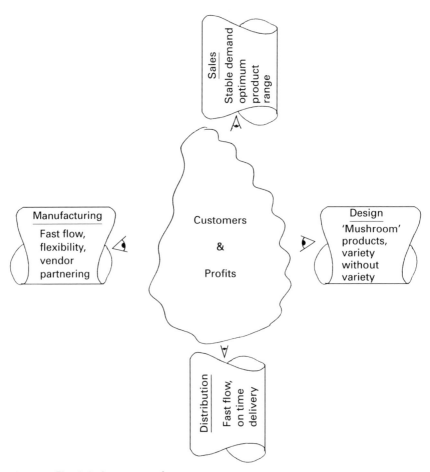

Fig. 2.6 A common focus.

Develop 'rock crushing' teams

Dramatic change is easy to talk about. Most people agree it is necessary and would benefit the business, but few are willing to accept dramatic change in *their* areas. This natural inertia comes from many sources. One is simply tradition – it has always been done that way. But 'tradition does not mean the living are dead, but that the dead are living'. It's time for those who are today walking around to 'take control'.

The best analogy I have seen to express the blockers to change is the river and rocks, one shown in Fig. 2.7. This picture came from the just-in-time (JIT) movement and is usually used to highlight factory problems. The analogy is a boat on a river. The level of water in the river (analogous to inventory levels) is high because of the rocks on the bottom. The level must be high to keep the boat clear of the rocks.

The rocks are all problems that need addressing. If they are reduced in size (crushed), water (inventory) levels can be reduced. This frees up assets, makes the process more flexible and reliable, reduces non value added work (NVAW) so reduces costs and results in better customer service.

But it is naive to believe that all the ills of a manufacturing company exist only in the factory operations. The other departments, such as sales, design and accounting, need the same in-depth analysis and critique to improve their performance.

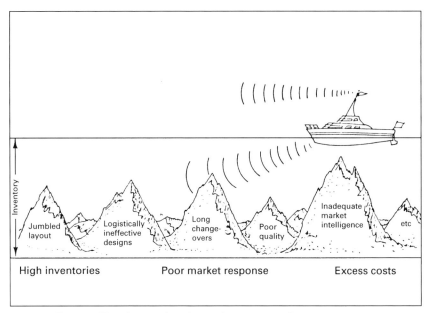

Fig. 2.7 The river and rocks analogy – operations.

Figure 2.8 is sales and marketing's river and rocks. This figure shows it's a complete misconception that sales and marketing are trying to profitably delight their customers. Nothing could be further from the truth. They have policies, procedures and actions that simultaneously increase inventories, increase costs and *reduce* customer service. They are the victims and culprits at the same time.

Figure 2.9 is design's river and rocks. The big problem here is that traditional ways of measuring the success of a design are completely wrong in

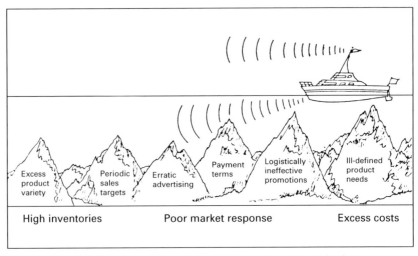

Fig. 2.8 The river and rocks analogy – sales and marketing.

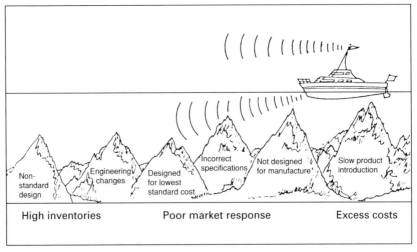

Fig. 2.9 The river and rocks analogy – design.

a buyers' market. Products must allow the plant to flex quickly to the dynamics of the market-place. They must also deliver excellent customer service with minimum assets. But such considerations – flexibility, customer service and assets – are rarely goals for designers. Functionality, product standard cost and aesthetics are the major guiding criteria.

I was going to give a picture of the river and rocks for accounting but I couldn't find a big enough piece of paper! Joking aside, it is obvious that all departments, including accounting, need this kind of treatment. All activities must be challenged against the objective of profitably delighting the customer. Crushing the rocks in all departments must be the action.

NVAW: huge controllable costs

I mentioned non-value-added-work or waste (NVAW) earlier. NVAW embraces all activities that take resources but do not add value to the customer or the business. NVAW is embodied in most of the rocks in the river but has other additional elements. Many processes have approval or check off requirements, especially accounting processes. These are analogous to inspection in the plant, obviously 100% NVAW. Lots of data published by your information system is completely useless and not used by anyone, so NVAW. Supervision is by definition NVAW.

Several companies have attempted to quantify the amount of NVAW in their businesses. Recognize this is not an easy project as some NVAW is very gray. For example, is a research and development (R&D) project that fails to develop a saleable product, NVAW? In simple terms, the answer is 'Yes' but, if this project created technology that will be used to make the next breakthrough product, the answer is 'No'.

The consensus opinion from these several companies is that NVAW is 40% of a company's sales! Recognize it cannot be made zero as some NVAW will always be present but reducing it in half in 12 to 18 months is certainly possible for most companies and I am sure the same is true for your company.

Business processing re-engineering challenges every activity and process against its role to add value. Huge decreases in activity and costs are possible using an open mind and determination to implement change.

3

Manage your planning dilemma: attack your P:D ratio

This concept, the P:D ratio, came from Shigeo Shingo's book, *Study of Toyota Production System*. The P:D ratio explains in simple terms one of the most difficult problems which manufacturers have to face – predicting and producing products prior to the customer's order. It also leads to the few solutions. The challenge is for you to think through these choices and pick the one or ones that will benefit your business the most.

What is 'P'?

Both 'P' and 'D' are lengths of time. 'P' is the length of time from ordering raw materials or purchased components, receiving them, processing them in your factory and shipping them to your customers. In other words, it is your internal procurement and manufacturing lead time. Figure 3.1 shows this diagrammatically for a fabrication and assembly business. I am sure people from other industries can substitute their terms and get the same understanding of what constitutes 'P'.

What is very important to realize is that some portion of these times is for storage of either materials or products in stockrooms, work in process (WIP) or warehouses. Hence 'P' time is the *average* length of time from ordering materials or components until the finished product containing the raw materials or components is shipped.

This same idea is shown pictorially in Fig. 3.2 for one of my clients in Brazil. They buy the raw materials in Europe, process them into components in one of their factories, also in Europe, ship these to Brazil where they are made into sub-assemblies in one factory and into finished products in another factory. The finished products are then sent through their distribution channel into the retail stores where the finished product is finally bought.

Figure 3.2 shows clearly the idea of 'P' time being an average because the variability is also shown. One product can always be expedited through

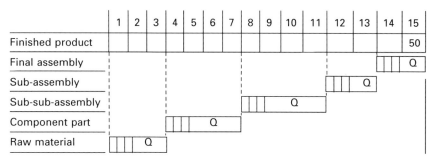

	1	2	3	4	5	6	7	8	9	10	11	12	13	14	15
Finished product															50
Final assembly															Q
Sub-assembly												Q			
Sub-sub-assembly							Q								
Component part					Q										
Raw material		Q													

Fig. 3.1 Lead time build-up – 'P'.

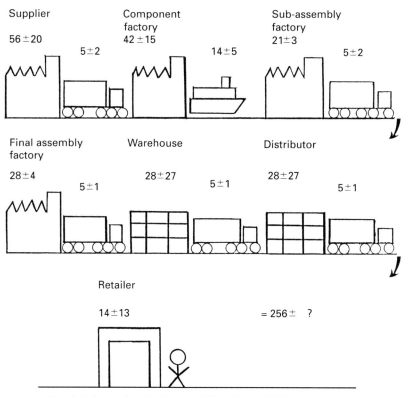

Fig. 3.2 Lead time build-up – 'P' with variability.

the production process, so shows a short 'P' time. But it is always at the expense of other products now set aside to make room for the expedited product. The set aside products will have longer 'P' times, so the average will not change.

Response 'P' time

Perhaps of more importance than the average 'P' time is the time it would take to respond to a market-place change. If the total demand jumped 20% overnight, how quickly could you respond and *maintain* a 20% increase in production? What if the mix of products sold changed dramatically? How fast could you change production of specifics to respond to and maintain this new selling mix?

These versions of 'P' time are attempting to quantify the flexibility of the business to respond to market dynamics. Make sure you realize these 'P' times are the time to react and *sustain* the change. Reacting quickly to a few orders and then having shortages or extending lead times to customers is not the way to profitably delight all your customers.

Why is variability important?

The variability of each element of 'P' time is shown in Fig. 3.2. It is obvious that this variability influences the predictability of replenishing inventory or delivering on time. High variability guarantees high inventories or poor customer service or, more likely, both at the same time. You'll never profitably delight customers with high variability. One way of attacking this variability is to reduce the total 'P' time, as described in several later chapters. The shorter the total, the narrower the variability.

Eli Goldratt in his book, *The Goal*, discusses many of the problems of process variability and ways to control it. Process variability and 'P' time variability are very similar concepts in that they both create the unpredictability that causes high inventories and shortages simultaneously. The solutions are also very similar.

What is 'D'?

'D' is the length of time from when a customer gives you an order until you ship. In fact, it can be four lengths of time:

D1 is the length of time you *tell* customers they have to wait for your products.

D2 is the length of time customers *wish* they had to wait for your products. This is often less than D1.

D3 is the length of time that would give you a competitive edge if you could reliably deliver at least a portion of your production in this length of time. D3 is often the same as D2 but in many cases, incremental business can be gained if you can reliably deliver some products on a very short lead time.

D4 is the *actual* time customers wait for your products. This is often longer than all the others, at least for a portion of your output. Your delivery performance, if less than 100%, tells you about D4.

Of course, D times will vary by product line and perhaps by distribution channel. Quantifying the four 'D's for each business segment will allow you to take the next step.

Defining your P:D ratio

The P:D ratio is simply P divided by D, as shown in Fig. 3.3. What is critically important to realize is there is no link between these two lengths of time. They are both independent variables. P is wholly under the control of the company and its relationship with its supply chain. D, especially D2 and D3, are what the customer or market-place wants.

Figure 3.3 shows P greater than D. This is true for almost all industries. Very few have P less than D. It's also true that customers are pushing D times to become shorter, thus increasing P:D ratios unless companies address their P times in some way.

Pick your decoupling points

The type of business you are in influences to a great degree how you plan and control your business. As a starting point, the inverted triangles in Fig. 3.4 show where you decouple your forecasted demand from the actual or known demand for a variety of industries.

In a make-to-stock company, all the 'P' time is based on forecasts or speculation. Products have to be made and placed on the shelf in the hope that someone will buy them. D is obviously very small in this case, instantaneous or a few hours at most. This is true if we are looking at the end

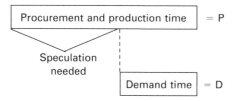

Fig. 3.3 P:D ratio.

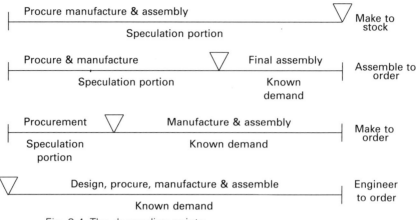

Fig. 3.4 The decoupling points.

customers' 'D' time. If we use the distributors' or retail stores' ordering time from the manufacturer, then D could be a week or more.

For an assemble-to-order company, only a portion of the 'P' time is based on speculation. The final assembly or configuration time is based on known customer demand.

For make-to-order, only procurement can be done based on speculation. The balance is based on known demand and usually involves some custom engineering that obviously adds to the total 'P' time.

For true engineer-to-order, nothing can be done ahead of the customer's order. Only after the order is received and the product designed can procurement and manufacture start. Design is obviously a key ingredient of 'P' time in this scenario.

The solution to your P:D ratio problem will be heavily influenced by what type of business you are in. Although all the solutions to the problem, described later in this chapter, will have some impact on the result, focus on those that will have major influence on your type of business.

Forecasting, speculation or gambling

When P exceeds D, as it does for the majority of industry, the difference must be filled in with forecasts. Predicting what customers want allows you to do all the necessary things before the customer's order arrives, up to the decoupling point. You can then deliver products in the balance of time.

I would like you to promise never to use the word 'forecasting' again when describing this problem of predicting what customers will buy. As you can see from Figures 3.3 and 3.4, I have chosen the word 'speculation'. This is because the word 'forecasting' doesn't convey the idea of financial risk that is being taken and a company takes a huge financial risk when P exceeds D. The commitment of cash to vendors for materials and, in most cases, for production of finished goods or an intermediate stage is all based on the premise you can forecast well. We all know that forecasts are either lucky or lousy! Fire sales of excess products, shortages of products customers want and excess and obsolete inventory are all indications of the problem.

A better term than speculation is 'gambling'. People involved in the predictive process for their business should be described as members of the 'gamblers club'. Why? Because maybe you bought the right materials, made the right products and customers bought them. You gambled and won. Maybe you bought the wrong materials, made the wrong products and customers didn't want them. You gambled and lost. And maybe you didn't buy the materials, you didn't make the products, but the customers want them. You gambled and lost again.

As you can see, you can gamble and win once, gamble and lose twice. And when you gamble and lose, you almost always lose twice at the same time – excesses of wrong things and shortages of right things. You can see the impact on your ROA and your ability to profitably delight your customers.

Understand your planning dilemma

This whole problem of predicting sales before the order has been received causes huge costs, excess assets and lost sales for most companies. The process can be seen in Fig. 3.5 for a manufacturer. On the left-hand side, forecasts are used to make output plans for the business. These forecasts set in motion the whole left-hand side activities of buying raw materials and manufacturing products over the P minus D time.

Some time later, at the start of the D time, a customer's order is received or the warehouse needs replenishing. If the left-hand side matches the right-hand side, in other words if your forecast matches the reality of the customer's order or the warehouse inventory, then the term 'intermediate inventory' is simply the decoupling point. No physical inventory exists. The left-hand side provides products that the right-hand side immediately consumes.

However, this assumes that your forecast is exactly correct. If it is not, then the simultaneous problems mentioned earlier of excess inventory and shortages occur. Now the term, 'intermediate inventory' is reality, there *is* inventory there, but it's the wrong stuff. Let's go back to our earlier dis-

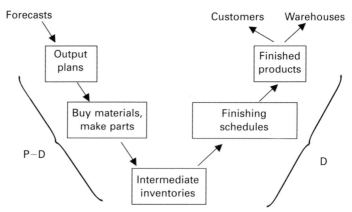

Fig. 3.5 The planning dilemma.

cussion of NVAW. If you make the wrong products, what percent of your business is NVAW? The answer is, 100%.

Of course, no company makes only wrong products, some percent are correct and are sold. But many companies make significant amounts of the wrong products. This has to be called NVAW and is the largest single element of controllable costs in many cases.

The distribution planning dilemma

Figure 3.6 shows the same process for distributors. They have to order products from their suppliers before the sale is made. This forecast or better yet, speculation, results in inventories ahead of the customer buying. If they forecast correctly, then inventories are very low and service is high. If they forecast wrongly, the twin evils of excess wrong inventories and shortages occur together.

Retailers have the same problem. The proliferation of stock reduction sales seen in most shopping centers are good indicators of their success or failure to manage their dilemma.

Three choices to solve the planning dilemma

The various detailed actions you can take to solve or mitigate the problems of the P:D ratio can be put into three groups, as follows:

1   Improve the plan. This means to work hard to make the left-hand side of the planning dilemma closer to the right-hand side. The ultimate objective is to make the left-hand side identical to the right-hand side.

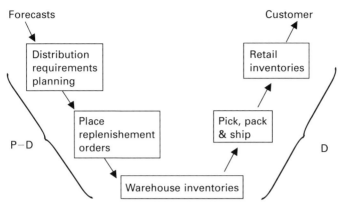

Fig. 3.6 The distribution planning dilemma.

2 Add contingency. Recognize that 'accurate forecasts' is an oxymoron so buffer the inherent error in forecasts in some way in your planning. This may increase your costs or assets. The hope is that serving customers well, so making the sale, will pay for these incremental expenditures.

3 Dynamically change the plan. What this means is to make an output plan and break it down into detailed plans for all elements in the bill of material or recipe. Start to execute them. You are now some amount into the 'P' time. Keep comparing this original output plan against your latest intelligence from the marketplace. If you sense the current plan is incorrect, then change the output plan to your latest market inputs. This now means revising all the detailed plans you are currently executing based on the original plan.

Correct versus actual priority

To establish the correct priority of these three choices, let's look at the risk and cost of each choice. If you can significantly improve the plan, you will be in a low cost and low risk situation. It's low cost because few schedule changes will be needed. It's low risk because you will make the right products. If you cannot improve the plan significantly, then adding contingency could mask the error from the customer. It is a high cost process to provide contingency, but it is low risk because you should be able to satisfy customers.

What if neither of these are done? Then keeping the plans dynamic with constant rescheduling of vendors and your operations is a choice. But this is high cost, paying for all the overhead people needed to manage this complex environment. It is also high risk because it only takes one vendor or one work center in your company not to respond and you cannot deliver.

Logic says therefore to attack the planning dilemma in the sequence just described. First, improve the plan as much as possible. If you can't make it perfect, then second, add contingency. Third, if these two actions cannot cope with the predictive problem, create a dynamically changing scheduling system.

This is *not* the way we have addressed the problem. We have usually gone at it in exactly the reverse way. Most companies have implemented computer programs based on manufacturing resource planning (MRP II) concepts that are used to dynamically change the plan. Nowhere near as much effort has gone into improving the plan or adding contingency.

Because of the effort most companies have already spent on dynamic replanning systems, I am not going to cover them. If you are in one of those companies you could probably teach me about rescheduling the reschedules you just rescheduled. Instead I will focus on the top two priorities: improving the plan and adding contingency.

Six ways to improve the plan

What I am focusing on is how to make the left-hand side of Fig. 3.5 closer to the reality of the right-hand side. Several of these ideas will also be valid for distributors and retailers, shown in Fig. 3.6. The ultimate objective is to make the left-hand side identical to the right-hand side. The six suggested ways are:

1 Reduce P time.
2 Force a match.
3 Increase D time.
4 Simplify the product line.
5 Standardize.
6 Forecast more accurately.

Reduce P time

One characteristic of forecasts is, the further out into the future you make them, the more wrong they are. Reducing the forecast horizon improves forecast accuracy. This horizon for product manufacture is dictated by the P time. The ultimate objective is to make P equal to or less than D. If this could be done, then you could eliminate all product speculations. You would be a make-to-order company. The strategic objective for every manufacturer should be to stop speculating. You would simultaneously reduce risk and increase your financial returns. (Reducing 'P' times will be covered in detail in Chapter 4.)

Force a match

There are two directions to solve the dilemma – make the left-hand side equal to the right or the right-hand side equal to the left. Making the left-hand side equal to the right means to manufacture what the market-place wants. Making the right-hand side equal to the left means to sell to the market-place what you have made.

Most people react negatively to this latter idea. They are conditioned to believe you should always make what customers want. But many companies force, or at least influence their customers to buy what they have. The smart ones do this and delight their customers profitably at the same time.

Restaurants are a good example of successfully forcing a match. Most have specials that are a little cheaper than their regular meals. What's a special in a restaurant? Yesterday's obsolete or excess inventory, of course. The special attracts buyers and the restaurant gets rid of what would otherwise be thrown away. The waiter also tells you what items on the menu are not available today. The excuse is that it is out of season or didn't look good at the market.

Most of us accept this behavior and are quite content to choose something else. So restaurants successfully force their customers to buy what they have and influence them to clean out any slow moving inventory.

Companies also use promotions to influence customers to buy what they have made. The problem with most promotions is that you delight customers but not profitably. We'll discuss promotions in more detail in Chapter 8.

Increase D time

The P:D ratio can be made much smaller with a larger D. The trick here is to be able to do this competitively, especially as most customers want shorter D times. A company in Texas making gas regulators has come up with a unique way of increasing D times at the same time as they profitably delight customers. Gas regulators are sold through distributors to licensed contractors. The manufacturer tells their distributors that, if they order this month for delivery in three months' time, they will get an incremental discount from the list price. If they order this month for delivery in less than three months, this discount does not apply. Approximately 80% of this company's customers' orders carry a three-month lead time. The balance is received with less than three months notice.

The manufacturer loves this system. He knows 80% of his business three months out, so can plan operations with great precision. These orders are very stable as the manufacturer limits the customers' ability to change these orders and still claim the incremental discount. Only 20% of their business needs the speculation process.

The customers, the distributors, also love this system. They agree they have to carry extra inventory because of ordering three months out but they say the incremental discount more than pays for the additional inventory carrying costs. They make a higher ROA when selling products bought on a three month order than a one month order. How's *that* for a win/win situation.

A white goods manufacturer in the UK was having trouble delivering on time to his customers, the discount chains and department stores. Discussions with his customers showed he was quoting the shortest lead time compared to his competitors. He felt that a short D was a competitive edge.

His customers explained they were more interested in *reliability* of delivery than the absolute length of time. They suggested he extend his D time if he would be more reliable. As soon as this change was made, his on-time delivery hit 100%. This performance set him apart from his competitors and was what delighted his customers. His costs and assets dropped because of his ability to both plan and execute better. How's that for profitably delighting your customers?

Simplify the product line

It is obvious that the wider variety of products you offer your customers, the more difficult it will be to make a good plan. The narrower the variety, the easier it will be to make a good plan. The laws of statistics guarantee these two statements are true.

Most sales and marketing people reading this section have probably switched me off after these assertions. A sales manager at one of my clients, after hearing me say this, reacted violently. He shouted: 'If you want an accurate plan, give me one product! Sales will be exactly zero! How's that for accuracy! If you want sales, give me some products!'

He was obviously correct. One product is probably not enough but infinity is certainly too many. The bounds are clear. How many products should we have? To do what? Profitably delight customers, of course. The key word is the first one and I will rephrase it as 'maximize the return on assets by delighting some customers'. The job is not to delight customers but maximize the financial results of the business.

This suggests that there is an optimum number of products we should offer. This optimum can be influenced by how we design products, the technology we use to control the business and how much we make versus buy and resell, but there will still be an optimum. What is the right number is the only question. This is true for distributors and retailers as well. There is an optimum variety they should offer their customers.

However, few companies offer an optimum variety of products. They have no way of calculating their optimum so use their gut feelings to manage their offerings or periodically go through major product rationalization programs. This is when it is obvious to everyone that they offer too many products. These programs, typically run every 5 years, make major reductions in a company's portfolio of products. But no one is sure that they delete the losers and keep the winners. And as soon as this program is finished, new products start being added to build up the portfolio until the next rationalization program is launched.

Chapters 6 and 7 will address the product variety issue in detail. Chapter 5 will explain how designers can provide application variety without product variety, a win/win situation for both customers and the company.

How many products would you *like* to have? The answer is 'one', provided this one product satisfies every application variety. Its standard cost would be a little higher to do this than application specific products but it would provide a higher ROA for the company because, if you had any products in stock, they would be the right ones so you would give excellent service. The assets needed to give this service would be miniscule and your actual costs, especially NVAW, would be low because of the simplicity of the business.

Getting multi-application products requires a clear design, sales and marketing strategy. Few companies have this, leading to the proliferation of products most companies are wrestling with today.

Standardize

I am applying this term to everything that happens prior to the decoupling point. For make-to-stock companies this is the same as simplifying the product line. For other companies it means to standardize raw materials, purchased components and whatever else they have to do while speculating. The more you can standardize, the lower the risk of forecast error. Product variety must now be added after the customer's order has been received.

How many raw materials or purchased components would you *like* to have? The answer is again 'one', as long as you can provide the product variety from this one ingredient that allows you to profitably delight your customers.

Clearly an ideal design strategy would be to provide product variety from a limited variety of raw materials or ingredients. This would be worthwhile even if these standard raw materials or ingredients had a somewhat higher standard cost than product specific materials. The reduced risk, lower assets and increased flexibility that standardization would provide would easily pay for some increased standard costs.

Few companies have such a design strategy clearly stated. Even worse, one of the key measurements designers use to select components and raw materials is their standard cost. They select those that give the lowest product standard cost, hence highest gross margin. But low standard cost and high margin do not guarantee the highest ROA. In fact, just the opposite. These narrow objectives usually guarantee you increased assets and reduced responsiveness to the market, hence a reduced ROA.

A design strategy is needed to ensure that the fewest raw materials and purchased components can be made into the necessary end product variety and this strategy must overpower the need for the lowest standard cost and highest margin. It must promote designing products to maximize ROA, a very different focus for designers.

Forecast more accurately

I know I said earlier that accurate forecasts is an oxymoron but it *is* possible to reduce forecast error. Creating a formal process to gather and analyze data from the field can make you aware of many previously hidden changes in customer preferences or buying plans. Routinely measuring actual sales against the forecast to identify errors and the source of these errors can allow you to make better predictions next time. Having a cross-functional team of people actively involved in the forecasting process makes sure all factors that could affect future sales are included.

It is obvious, however, that the law of diminishing returns applies to forecasting. Significant incremental effort at some time makes only marginal improvements in the forecast accuracy. It is also true that the earlier suggestions to solve the P:D ratio problem could make the forecasting problem easier or take away the need for product forecasts altogether. Make sure you explore all the potential of the previous five ways to improve the plan before you spend a lot of effort on this one. The best forecast you ever made was the one you didn't need to make. Try to get out of the speculation problem to reduce risk and increase ROA. It will pay off a lot better than working on forecast accuracy.

Two ways to add contingency

The prior six ways to improve the plan will make the plan better, meaning it will be closer to reality. But it may not be exactly the same – customers still are not reading and buying to your forecast. At this stage, it may be worthwhile to buffer the error in the forecast in some way. It means being willing to spend additional money or carry additional assets to be able to respond to the customers' needs.

Safety stock

Safety stock could be additional finished goods, raw materials, purchased components or semi-finished products, additional to your expected requirements. It is an amount of inventory deliberately set aside to take care of demand variability.

Does it work? I often ask people in my seminars: 'Who has safety stock somewhere in their company?' Most hands go up. I then ask: 'Who has factory shortages and back orders to customers?' Again, most hands go up. Now wait a minute. Safety stock but no shortages or back orders is logical. No safety stock but shortages or back orders is also logical. But safety stock *and* shortages or back orders is *illogical*.

What's the problem? For safety stock to work you must first be able to forecast how *inaccurately* you can't forecast, for the item in question. Now you can calculate, to two decimal places if you like, how much additional inventory you need to keep you out of trouble based on your forecast of how inaccurately you can't forecast. Science at work!

As my little test proves time and time again, safety stock rarely works. There are only a few times when forecast error is predictable by item. In these cases, safety stock can be an excellent investment. For the others, the majority, safety stock provides the worst return on assets you can imagine.

Overplanning

Overplanning is a technical term that means to plan extra capacity, over and above what is necessary to produce your expected requirements. This extra capacity must be linked to the type of forecast error you are experiencing.

Forecast error is a two dimensional problem. First, you can forecast the volume well but you cannot forecast the mix. Getting the mix right is the primary forecasting problem. It accounts for about 95% of forecast error. Second, you can't forecast the volume well. This is a rare forecasting problem, accounting for the balance of 5% of forecast error.

Mix errors

The impact on capacity from mix errors in the forecast is a function of the process configuration in the plant. Assume three dedicated processes. Line A makes product family A. There is a wide variety of specific products in this family but they must all be made on line A.

Line B makes (you guessed it) product family B. Again, there is a wide variety of specific products in this family but they must all be made on line B. The same story is true for line C. You cannot make product family A products on line B or C and vice versa.

Where must you have excess capacity to respond to your largest forecast error problem – mix? On the equipment that is mix sensitive, of course, which means on all three lines which, on average, will be 100% idle. If product line A sells more, assuming we have forecast the volume well, then lines B and C sell less so, on average, the additional capacity is always idle.

Compare this to one processing line that can make A, B or C products with minimal change-over. Now where must you have excess capacity to respond to a mix problem? The answer is nowhere. It's a scheduling problem, not a capacity problem. Schedule more As, less Bs or Cs and the mix issue is handled.

Let me state up front, I know it is impossible, from a practical perspective, to make all products on one processing line. But is it not also clear that dedicated lines take a scheduling problem (mix forecast error) and make it a capacity problem? Which would you rather have, a scheduling problem or a capacity problem? The obvious answer is a scheduling problem. What processes would you *like* to have in your factory? The answer is one line of equipment that can make any product, any time, with minimal change-overs. This may not be the most efficient but it would be the most flexible and probably contain the lowest assets, hence ROA would be enhanced.

What am I cautioning you against? Dedicated lines, their justification based on small improvements in efficiency. Challenge all dedicated equipment. Make sure the payback is large and fast. Recognize that dedicated lines in a market-place with forecast mix problems are potentially the worst investment you could possibly make.

Volume errors

Whether you have one line or ten dedicated lines, if you have a volume forecast error, you must have additional excess capacity everywhere to respond to it. This excess could be in the form of overtime, turned on or off to suit the real demand. It could be with a subcontract source that can pick up your overloads during peak times. Here volume forecast error is a true capacity problem that can only be solved with flexible capacity.

The P:D ratio problem needs a multifaceted solution

Reflect on the six ways of improving the plan and the two ways of adding contingency. It is easy to see that only a cross-functional attack on the problem will give satisfactory results. No one department can solve this alone.

This cross-functional approach is shown in Fig. 3.7. The various solutions are listed vertically, the key departments horizontally. The X in each box shows the *primary* responsibility to address this solution. As you can see, there are some shared responsibilities. Cross-functional teams will be needed to address these issues successfully.

I have shown the primary responsibilities. No question, you could argue that more cross-functional processes than are shown are necessary. I agree. The only problem is, if every box has an X in it, the chart loses value. I believe the Xs in the chart show the primary responsibilities. The identified departments must take the lead in any program to address these issues. It's the only way you will make significant steps to solve your P:D ratio problem.

Choice	Dept responsible		
	Mfg	Eng	Sales
Reduce P time	×	×	
Extend D time			×
Standardize product		×	
Simplify product line		×	×
Force a match			×
Forecast more accurately			×
Add contingency	×		×

Fig. 3.7 P:D ratio solutions.

Co-ordination through the S&OP process

Sales and operations planning (S&OP) is a process with two distinctly different roles to address your P:D ratio problem. The first is co-ordination. Manufacturing companies are usually broken up into different business functions, such as sales, accounting, design and manufacturing. Each of these functions has its own set of goals and objectives that are set, usually annually, during the strategic planning sessions.

This process aligns strategic direction at the macro level. At a more detailed level, the day-to-day running of the business, the necessary alignment of goals just doesn't happen. Conflicts can and do occur that get in the way of profitably delighting customers.

This is what is known as a disconnect. Nothing links the strategic direction of the business to its day-to-day operations. It's not surprising, then, that many senior managers, at each annual strategic meeting, start off by wondering why last year's strategic objectives weren't met.

Lots of factors affect how the day-to-day business is run. Many of these are external to the business, such as customer demand, the economy, competitors' actions, supplier falldowns, etc. Some are internal, such as a delayed new product launch, financial issues, serious capacity shortfalls and so on.

Success in the market-place can only occur when all business functions are working together in concert to solve these operating problems. You cannot get speed of response to customer needs, availability of product when required or any other customer desired characteristic if all functions are not playing the same tune. Discord is the inevitable result.

These musical terms have led the S&OP process to be likened to a symphony orchestra creating wonderful music. The musical score ensures everyone is playing the same tune, the conductor guarantees all orchestra sections play at the same speed. Working the S&OP process performs the same functions for a manufacturing company. The output plan, shown in Figures 2.4 and 2.5, is the deliverable from this role of the S&OP process. This plan is the key driver of all subsequent actions throughout the company.

The second role of the S&OP process is to create actions that will help make the business more competitive. These are the actions shown in Fig. 3.7 plus any others that are identified. The cross functional nature of most competitive issues requires that the necessary actions are reviewed and co-ordinated centrally.

The sales and operations planning (S&OP) process defined

APICS, the American Production and Inventory Control Society, defines S&OP this way: 'S&OP is a process that provides management the ability to strategically direct its businesses to achieve competitive advantage on a continuous basis by integrating customer-focused marketing plans for new and existing products with the management of the supply chain. The process brings together all the plans for the business (sales, marketing, development, manufacturing, sourcing and financial) into one integrated set of plans. It is performed at least once a month and is reviewed by management at an aggregate (product family) level. The process must reconcile all supply, demand, and new product plans at both the detail and aggregate level and tie them to the business plan. It is the definitive statement of the company's plans for the near to intermediate term covering a horizon sufficient to plan for resources and support the annual business planning process. Executed properly, the sales and operations planning process links the strategic plans for the business with its execution and reviews performance measures for continuous improvement.'

The process in a nutshell

The main focus of the S&OP process is a meeting, held monthly, chaired by the general manager, with the heads of each business function present, along with key middle managers and support staff. Their first job is to review the past month's performance from an operational sense, that is, customer service levels, inventory status, lead times to customers, forecast accuracy, etc, and then to review the resulting financial performance. This review of the past is to provide a base from which to predict the future.

The second job is to approve definitive plans for the future conduct of the business. These plans will have been worked out by the middle managers and staff at pre-S&OP meetings. As long as there are no problems, the S&OP meeting will simply endorse these plans. Where there are problems, such as a capacity constraint, scarce materials, a delayed new product launch, etc, then the various alternatives to solve these problems are presented. The senior managers must now select the best alternative which becomes the operating plan for the business.

The third job is to review the status of existing actions or initiate new ones to improve the competitiveness of the business.

Data gathering and scheduling are critical

The S&OP process is all about data presentation, either data about past performance or that related to the future. This data may not be available in the best format or at the correct level of detail for ease of discussion so must be reformatted. Several different people in different business functions have to work with this data to provide meaningful input to the S&OP deliberations, such as sales people creating forecasts, materials people converting forecasts to production plans, analyzing capacity requirements, etc.

Because of this interdependency of data and the large amount of it that needs to be worked, it is critical that a schedule of S&OP events be created several months into the future. This schedule must define exactly when raw data is to be available, when it will be worked into its various forms, when the pre-S&OP meetings are held and, finally, when the S&OP meeting will be conducted. Without this rigid discipline, the S&OP process will deteriorate into opinions and assumptions, not facts. As such is it doomed.

Back-to-basics management

There is nothing exotic about the S&OP process. It is a basic way of running the business. Surprisingly, though, many companies do not use it. Not surprisingly, these latter companies rarely get excellent results.

The resistance to using the process comes from two misconceptions. Firstly, we don't have time for all this data gathering, manipulation and meetings, and it does take time. Secondly, we (senior managers) know how to run our departments. We don't need one more meeting to make sure we are doing our jobs right.

But where else should you spend your time, other than in running the business better? And, as mentioned earlier, it is easy at the operational level for different departments to be working at cross purposes to each other. It will be hard to profitably delight customers with this lack of a concerted effort to solve business problems and improve the competitive posture of the company. Those companies that have bought into the process, many of them reluctantly, have come to believe it is the *only* way to run a business. All business functions use the same musical score (operating plan) and the conductor (general manager) ensures they are all playing at the same speed. Beautiful music (business results) is the outcome.

4

Making manufacturing more flexible

I have yet to find a company that does not have a dynamic market-place. Even companies that engineer products to order, so theoretically have a stable demand, find their customers routinely change schedules and specifications, hence they need to accommodate these changes and still deliver when the customer needs the product. Flexibility is the key to excellent customer satisfaction and low assets simultaneously. It is a mandatory condition to profitably delight your customers, regardless of the type of product or process.

Six causes of inflexibility and their solutions

Most of the major reasons preventing a company from being very flexible can be seen in the river and rocks analogy of Fig. 2.7.

The six major problems are as follows:

1 Layout.
2 Change-overs.
3 Unpredictable problems.
4 Systems.
5 Organization.
6 Measurements.

I will cover each of them in turn and explain how to crush each 'rock' for dramatic flexibility gains.

Layout

Factories were traditionally laid out with each technical specialty grouped together. This is shown in Fig. 4.1. It is called a functional layout. The example is from a machine shop. I trust those from other industries can replace these machining terms with their own. The concept is that technical expertise in each process is the key to success so all, like technical opera-

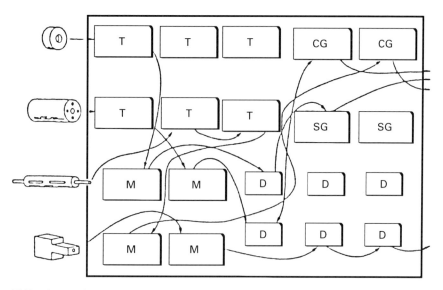

T–Turning equipment
M–Milling equipment
D–Drilling equipment
CG–Centerless grinding
SG–Surface grinding

Fig. 4.1 A functional layout.

tions are grouped in the same area under the same supervision and operated with people expert at this one technical specialty.

Look at the flow paths this generates. To make any one product, it must pass through several of the technical specialty departments. The throughput time of any job will be a function of how much other work is in these various departments and their competition for the same resources. Scheduling this complex environment will be complicated, maybe impossible. Work-in-process inventory will be high because of the queues of jobs waiting to be processed at bottleneck resources. Actual throughput times will be long and variable.

Responsibility and accountability are unclear

In the functional layout, who is responsible for the quality of the completed product? The answer is 'everybody', everybody who performed any of the technical operations to make the product. But another name for everybody is nobody. Clear responsibility and accountability if the product is found to be defective or sub-standard does not exist.

The same is true about schedule adherence. Who is responsible to make sure this product is completed when the customer needs it? Everybody and nobody again. Who is responsible and accountable to improve the total process, encompassing all the technical areas? The answer here is worse than everybody and nobody, because parochial behavior will guarantee no one looks at the total process. Walls between functions will block an overall look. Some improvements might be made in each functional area but these will probably sub-optimize the total process.

This layout guarantees a fragmented approach to production and a lack of accountability. It guarantees inflexibility, although theoretically it is the most flexible layout, because of the over specialization this form of layout creates.

From functional to cellular arrangements

The alternative to a functional layout, with machines grouped by their specialty, is a cellular layout. Here, machines are grouped by product or component type they make. This means different types of equipment are grouped together, as shown in Fig. 4.2.

A good analogy is that a functional layout is like a downtown traffic pattern. Pathways cross, bottlenecks occur, travel is slow and erratic. A cellular layout is like a highway, with all traffic moving in the same direction. Travel is fast and predictable.

Responsibility and accountability is clear in a cell layout, for both quality and schedule. The total process is visible to the operators who now work as a team to improve *their* process. Scheduling cells is straightforward. The cell functions as one large machine, not as each machine individually. Schedule work in the starting work center in the correct sequence and jobs must be completed in the same sequence.

The throughput time will be fast and predictable, mainly because of the elimination of queues of work typically found in a functional layout.

Requirements for flexible cells

Quick change-overs, covered a little later in this chapter, are mandatory. Long change-overs on any one machine will block the flow of work, making all machines in the cell idle. Long change-overs also force large batches to be made, to amortize the set-up costs or because of capacity limitations. These large batches tie up the cell for long periods of time so it is no longer available to react quickly to the latest customer needs.

Cross training of the cell operators, so everyone is proficient to operate all machines in their cell, is also necessary so absenteeism doesn't mean shutting one machine down, thus closing down the cell. This also helps to balance the workload among all operators as the mix or volume of products needed to be produced fluctuates. Lastly, it is to make everyone aware

Group layout (flow-line cell)

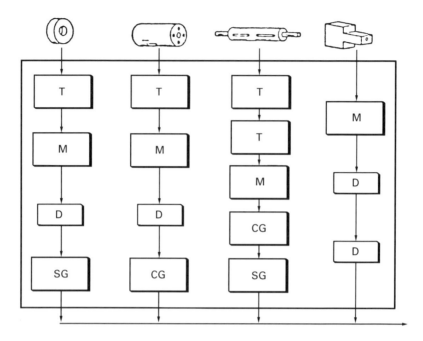

T–Turning equipment
M–Milling equipment
D–Drilling equipment
CG–Centerless grinding
SG–Surface grinding

Fig. 4.2 A cellular layout.

of all processes occurring in the cell to get a concentrated effort on process improvements.

Cautions for cells

A given layout of equipment is optimum for a certain volume and mix of production. Change the volume and/or mix and the layout is wrong. Cells are especially vulnerable to this problem as they are deliberately set up to make a given volume of a given product range. To overcome this deficiency, make sure the machines in the cells are on wheels, figuratively or in reality. By this, I mean to ensure that machines can be easily moved into new configurations of cells or into the same cells but with different volume capabilities. Be prepared to go through this physical rearrangement whenever the volume or mix of production has changed significantly.

Another concern expressed by many people is that cells require companies to purchase additional capital equipment. The logic is that in cells, all machines produce at the rate dictated by the slowest machine in the cell. All machines that could operate faster than this, therefore, have idle wasted capacity. This capacity may have been well utilized in a functional layout. Hence the need for additional equipment.

There is nothing wrong with this logic. Indeed, some companies have purchased additional machinery when making the transition to cells. Offsetting this capital expenditure, of course, is usually a significant reduction in work-in-process inventory, hence asset turnover is not badly affected.

Many companies find that process improvements in the cells create additional capacity that offsets the problem of slowing faster machines down to the slowest. Some companies have even been able to sell excess machines created by the process improvements stimulated by the cell arrangement.

Manufacturing cell advantages

Figure 4.3 lists the benefits of a cellular layout *vis-à-vis* a functional layout. The items on the left all increase, those on the right decrease. Some of these are only true if the cell is structured, operated and managed as close to an autonomous, entrepreneurial unit as is possible. Even so, those operated more traditionally still gain huge benefits from this transition.

Create cellular offices too

Cellular layouts have been applied to many factories but rarely to offices, but aren't office departments the same as specialized groupings of machines, in effect a functional layout? We have the order entry department, the credit checking department, scheduling department, engineering department, sales department and so on. The same problems of long and

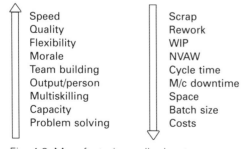

Fig. 4.3 Manufacturing cell advantages.

erratic information lead times, little responsibility and accountability for quality or schedule adherence and no focus on the total process are as evident in functionally oriented offices as in the plant. Creating cross functional groups of people grouped around a process creates cells out of office activities with equal, if not better, results than in the plant.

Change-overs

I use the terms, 'change-over', 'set-up' or 'make ready' interchangeably to describe the actions of converting a manufacturing process from making one item to making another. In some industries, this involves removing one set of tooling and replacing it with another. In others, it involves cleaning the process thoroughly of the old product to prepare for the new.

Some processes, after being stopped for change-over and then restarted, need a period of time of running before their performance parameters stabilize. Some amount of scrap or below grade products are produced before good product is finally obtained. The traditional way of addressing this problem is to run a large enough batch of product to amortize the change-over time and any resulting scrap. Hence change-overs are infrequent and resisted as much as possible.

The accounting system also favors large infrequent batches. Change-overs are indirect hours, running time is direct hours. Indirect hours cause overheads, direct hours absorb overheads, so the pressure is to have run hours, not change-over hours, resulting in many supervisors deliberately running more of a product than the schedule requires. Their operating performance, as defined by accounting, gets a boost every time they do this.

The solution is no solution at all

The science of calculating an economic run size to amortize the cost of the change-over was first published in 1915. The theory said there was a trade-off between the cost of the change-over and the holding cost of the inventory that a batch would cause. Create a large enough batch and the problem of expensive change-overs goes away.

But it doesn't go away. This theory simply transfers a problem from one place to the next, causing other problems in the process. High change-over costs are a problem for the plant. In some cases, change-overs could even cause a bottleneck and so have capacity implications. Running larger batches less frequently solves the change-over cost and capacity problems nicely, but now the problem sits in inventory. It hasn't gone away, it's just been relocated.

Large infrequent batches guarantee inflexibility. If a customer needs a product but you are running a large batch of another one, the customer has to wait. Large infrequent batches increase your speculative risk. Not only must you predict what customers need over the replenishment lead time but also over the depletion time of the batch. In essence, the batch size increases the total P time.

There are many other disadvantages of producing large batches such as, if a quality problem is found, you either have a large amount of rework or a large amount of scrap. In fact, I have been unable to find any advantages of large change-overs or large batches. They hurt every business wherever they are present.

Seven steps to quick changeovers

I will give you the methodology that I use when working with clients to reduce change-over time. Please follow it exactly if you wish to be successful with your own improvement program. But first, let's define what is meant by reducing change-over time. It means to reduce every incidence of change-over time, when converting from a given product A to another product B, C, D, etc.

Why I define it this way is because some people think it means reducing the total time the company spends on change-overs. This is just not true. The objective is to spend the same total time on change-overs but dramatically increase the frequency of change-overs, as shown in Fig. 4.4. Do this by reducing the time spent on each change-over.

I would only reduce the total time spent on change-overs if the piece of equipment is a true bottleneck. Then, reducing each incidence of change-over will free up capacity that will result in increased plant output.

Step one: select key players
Reducing change-over times is a continuous improvement activity. Some large gains can be made early in the process but, after this, it's small changes that add up over time to significant improvement.

The continuous improvement process dictates that the operators of the equipment take the lead in reducing change-overs. They are the only ones present continuously enough to work on change-over reduction. Technical people should be available in a support role. Their job is to verify the feasibility and then help implement the ideas coming from operator teams. This does not mean technical people cannot also contribute ideas to the change-over reduction process, of course they can. But technical people are project oriented. This is not a project but a series of incremental small

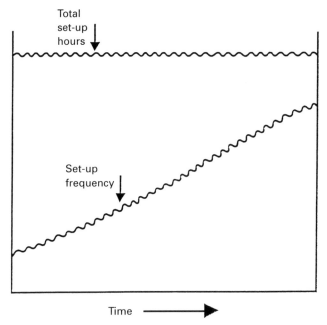

Fig. 4.4 Set-up performance.

improvements that can only be developed by the people intimately involved with the process.

Step two: conduct training programs

At least three types of training program are necessary. First, train the operators in team dynamics and problem solving. Such things as Pareto analysis, fishbone diagrams and brainstorming should be included.

Second, train them in how to conduct meetings. Include creating an agenda, staying focused, creating action items and how to follow-up to make sure the action items are completed.

Third, educate them on the technical issues related to quick change-overs. Explain the process of analysing today's methods, what key items to look for and provide case studies of successful change-over reductions with the before and after conditions explained.

Step three: set the objectives

As a minimum ask for 75% reduction in change-over times from today's best times. This extreme objective is for two reasons. First, you need this amount of reduction to get a significant increase in flexibility. Second, you are firmly stating that the process must change. You won't get this amount of improvement by everyone working harder. You nip in the bud the rumor it's another 'whip the operators' ploy.

Now tell them you don't have any money to spend on the improvements. They must come up with no-cost ideas. You do this to prevent wild suggestions, such as sell the equipment and buy a new machine, computerize the process, use a robot, etc. Especially tell the technical people you have no money. They are often quick to suggest an investment approach to gaining improvements. Tell them it's a brainpower approach you need and only after all these ideas are exhausted will you consider additional investment.   .

Step four: document and time the existing changeover procedure
This can be done one of two ways. First, give each team member a pad, pen and access to a clock or watch. Have another team member make the change-over. Simply have each team member write down the activities that occurred and how long each one took. Second, set up a video camera equipped with an elapsed time clock feature. Video tape the existing procedure.

In some companies, the idea of timing operator activities brings negative connotations because of the past history of sweat shops and speeding up assembly lines too fast for people to sustain. This has to be addressed head-on. You have to know how long various actions take now to figure out whether they are worth improving and by how much. Talk this out with those objecting to the timing activities. Find a solution that meets the needs of where are we now, what needs to change and have we made progress?

Step five: analysis and brainstorming
Use Pareto analysis to identify which activities consume large amounts of time. Focus everyone on these large chunks of time and brainstorm ways of reducing them. Three conditions typically result in a long time being taken.

1   Threaded fasteners used for clamping must be completely removed and then reinstalled. Modify the clamping system to completely eliminate the need for threaded fasteners or for them to turn a maximum of a half turn to clamp or unclamp.

2   Too few people performing the changeover. Frequently, adding people to the change-over process speeds it up greatly. This is similar to the difference between one person making up a king-size bed and two people doing it. With one person there is a lot of wasted motion. With two, the process is much more efficient. Check you have the right

change-over crew size, have everyone clear on their duties and organize the sequence of activities to minimize the total change-over time.

3   Too much time being spent adjusting the process to make a good product. Devise repeatable positioning devices to eliminate adjustments. Have set points on gauges, dials, etc, so that when a given product is being made you go immediately to these set points. Not only will this reduce the change-over time but it will also reduce the amount of start-up scrap.

Step six: routine measurement and display
Establish charts beside the equipment where change-over time is important. 'You can't control what you do not measure' is an old management adage. Have the operators report the times they experience on every set-up. Look to see a steady reduction in the time taken, perhaps with a step-wise change after a new idea has been implemented. Reward progress with recognition in the company newspaper, on the bulletin board and in employee meetings. Make sure the operators realize this is a program vital to the success of the company. It is one of the foundations to profitably delighting customers.

Step seven: standardize
Many times people make improvements, but over time they slip back to their old, comfortable ways of doing things. Any gains that were made are now lost. To offset this, have the operators document their latest and best way of performing various change-overs. Have these instructions available at all times in the area for reference.

This is especially necessary for multiple shift operations. Make sure all shifts perform each change-over the same way. Not only will you get the same speed each time, you will also get consistency of product output. Different ways of setting up machines has been proven to be the cause of most variability in product output.

Unpredictable problems

All manufacturers experience problems that interfere with their plans to make products to schedule. These problems have been called Murphy problems after the infamous Murphy's Law. They cause inflexibility in three ways. Say the problem is an unexpected machine breakdown or late vendor delivery. Firstly, these problems wreak havoc on specific production schedules and perhaps even customer deliveries. Not only is the current product affected but so are all other products that will use this machine or that need the material that is late.

Secondly, these problems steal capacity that could be used to respond to all customers better. Thirdly, people responsible for scheduling or quoting deliveries to customers always cushion their dates because of the unpredictable problems they are sure will be encountered. The only issue is, which problem will occur, when will it occur and what will be affected when it does? Facing these imponderables, you can guess at the amount of padding that goes on.

Actual performance when Murphy strikes confirms the scheduling people are correct to be unresponsive to customer needs. Delivery performance in an environment of high levels of unpredictable problems is obviously poor. No one is going to go out on a limb in this environment.

There are many unpredictable problems other than the two mentioned earlier. Quality problems, absenteeism, incorrect inventory records, engineering changes, and so on all add a level of uncertainty into the business. Flexibility is a pipe dream in these conditions.

Boot out 'Murphy'

No, you can't completely eliminate all Murphy's administrations but you can certainly reduce them enough to make them a non-issue. Here is where a lot of the recent alphabet soup techniques come into play. Machine breakdowns can be reduced through total preventative maintenance (TPM). Quality problems reduce dramatically with total quality management (TQM). Vendor delivery performance improves significantly with vendor partnering. (This particular issue, vendor partnering, will be dealt with in more detail in Chapter 9.) Just-in-time (JIT) pulls many of these techniques together into an overriding concern for process repeatability.

None of this, of course, is easy. It takes determination, a focus on the details and the belief that big improvements in process repeatability are possible.

Systems

Most manufacturing companies today use huge integrated systems to co-ordinate the activities of each facet of their business. These systems interact with large databases describing the product, how it is made, what inventories are present and available for future sales or production and so on. For the operations side of the business, these systems are based on concepts embodied in manufacturing resource planning (MRP II).

The outputs of these systems are schedules – for production of components, sub-assemblies and end products and for procurement of raw materials, parts, etc. Inputs are booked orders and forecasts of future sales, converted into a master production schedule.

These systems are periodic, meaning that changes or updates are processed on a fixed schedule, perhaps weekly or daily. This is because of the huge amount of data that must be processed to reflect a change, plus the time required for people to process the resulting detailed schedule revisions.

The result is what has been termed a 'push' system. Schedules are issued to vendors and to every factory work center based on the latest knowledge of customer demand and the factory conditions. If something suddenly changes, such as the receipt of a new customer order or an unpredicted factory disruption, the schedules that were originally issued are no longer valid. But they will remain in place until the next scheduled system run unless someone manually overrides the computer generated schedules. This time lag between an event and new schedules being issued can be up to a week. With customers requiring deliveries of products in days, such a time lag is completely unacceptable.

Make information liquid

In Chapter 2 I explained the need for a 'liquid' factory, with raw materials flowing into the plant, being transformed and flowing out of the plant as finished products to customers. Information can also be visualized as liquids flowing.

Figure 4.5 follows on from Fig. 2.5. In this case, information is flowing from the market-place into the company and back through pipes to the vendors. This information states the total demand on the company (rate) plus the sequence of deliveries specific customers want of specific quantities of specific products. The total demand is conceptualized as the diameter of the pipes, the specific deliveries as the numbers 4, 3, 2, 1.

Utopia would be instantaneous transmission to all affected areas of the business of the latest rate and sequence required by customers. The benefits are shown on the figure.

'Invisible' inventories are any pieces of information in the company related to producing or shipping products. For example, a customer order booked but not yet released for manufacture, could be thought of as invisible inventory. A better concept is costs incurred when designing a new product. These costs will not be recovered until you start selling the new

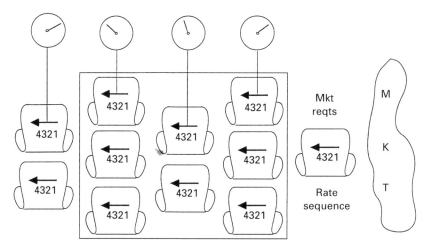

Low 'invisible' inventories
Short information lead times
High flexibility/responsiveness

Fig. 4.5 'Liquid' information.

product, so could be thought of as flowing into inventory. In reality, it is only a quirk of accounting that calls physical things we buy or make 'inventory' whereas ideas, data and concepts are expensed. In my opinion, many companies would gain a lot more value by reducing their invisible inventories than their physical, visible inventories. And many times, reducing the invisible inventory will also reduce the visible.

Fast flowing information

Many new technologies have speeded up the flow of information. Electronic data interchange (EDI) and FAX machines allow companies to send scheduling and payment information to each other almost instantaneously. Contrast this with any national mail service! Computer aided design (CAD) systems that are compatible between companies can send engineering, tooling and test data to each other, again almost instantaneously.

The slow down is not in the transmission of data, it is in the processing or gathering of the data prior to the transmission or acting on the data after it has been received. As mentioned earlier, most manufacturing control systems process their changes periodically. This is where the delay occurs.

Kanban

This is a Japanese word that literally translates into 'card'. It now stands for a technique that was developed to get manufacturing companies to respond more quickly to customer demand.

The process is shown simplistically in Fig. 4.6. Operator A can select a variety of raw materials stored within his work area and manufacture a variety of components. These are placed near operator B. Operator B can select from the variety of components and manufacture a variety of sub-assemblies. These are placed near operator C. Operator C can select from the variety of sub-assemblies to make a variety of finished goods which are then sent directly to a customer or into finished goods inventory.

The inventory ahead of each operator is divided into two pieces, the minimum and the maximum. Typically these would be expressed in hours of average consumption, such as 1 hour minimum, 2 hours maximum. All operators have the same instructions: 'When all items are above their minimum, stop work. Only work when an item's minimum has been reached and then produce only enough to reach the maximum'.

The trigger for production is a customer's order or an item in finished goods inventory has reached its minimum. Operator C is immediately authorized to start producing the needed item. He withdraws the necessary sub-assemblies from his stock which may cause some to reach their minimum. Operator B now is authorized to produce more of these sub-

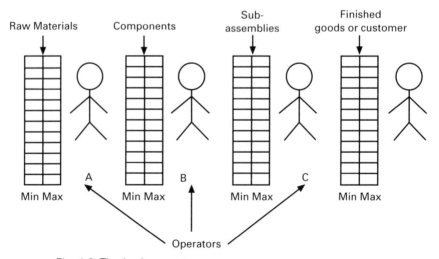

Fig. 4.6 The kanban system.

assemblies. She withdraws components, perhaps causing some to reach their minimum. Operator A now springs into action. This can be extended back to vendors who replenish the pertinent raw materials when any reach their minimum.

The card (Kanban) is simply the communication vehicle that an item has reached its minimum and needs replenishing. No card is required when the operators can visually see the minimums, maximums and current levels of inventory in their areas.

Compare this technique with a periodic planning system, described earlier such as MRP II. With Kanban, as each customer order is received or each finished goods item reaches its minimum, operator C gets notification of the need. His current workload from prior orders will determine how fast he reacts to this new demand. Typically, if the capacity of this work center has been sized correctly, he will be responding in an hour or so. All feeding work centers will also respond quickly to this order, the time lag a function of the specific minimums and maximums set on their inventory items.

Is it a panacea? – of course not. This technique works exceptionally well when demand is repetitive for similar items and the demand is fairly constant. Not all companies have this type of demand pattern in total but most companies have it for some portions of their business. Apply the technique where it makes sense. It eliminates a lot of routine planning and scheduling. Focus your people now on the more erratic, non-repetitive demand where judgment, plus a fast acting system, are the solution.

Organization

I touched on this problem earlier during the discussion of cells. Most companies are still organized in a command and control hierarchy. Each business specialty, such as sales, design, manufacturing, accounting and so on have their head person, often a vice president, reporting to the president or general manager. Each specialty then collects all the people related to that business function and organizes them vertically with senior managers, middle managers, supervisors and employees.

This form of organization is excellent for vertical communications up and down the organization. It is poor for horizontal communications between the various specialties. But products flow horizontally as shown in Fig. 2.5. Factory cells are groups of people all focused on moving the product from raw material to the customer so could be called a horizontal organization. The members of the cell are cross trained in all jobs in that area so they can quickly flex to varying work loads.

Information should also flow horizontally, as shown in Fig. 4.5. But with a vertical organization, information halts at the boundaries between specialties and frequently the information now travels vertically, up and down the specialty department's organization. It does not move quickly from the marketplace through the company and off to the vendors as Fig. 4.5 requires.

Go with the flow

Firms should be organized around the flow of product or information. This has been called business process re-engineering (BPR). The word 'process' comes into the picture because it also represents a flow of information from the initiating element to the closing element.

Group people both physically and organizationally around a process. Make sure they are cross trained, at least in the routine parts of each specialty department's activities. Focus their attention on speed – how long does the process take from the initiating element to the closing element? Drive this time down and see the resulting increase in flexibility this provides, especially with processes such as order entry that are related to customer demand.

Measurements

The recent transition from a seller's to a buyer's market has made many of our past performance indicators useless. In fact, many are worse than useless, they are downright dangerous to the health of the company.

In a seller's market, internal measures of performance are adequate. Such things as machine utilization, direct labor efficiency and variances to standard were considered the keys to success. What was missed was the fact that these measures rewarded individual people or departments, not teams of people or the business in total. It also resulted in large inventories, hiding NVAW and quality issues. JIT was the process that revealed these negatives of past performance measures.

Of even more importance is the problem that measurements that may suit a seller's market are completely wrong in a buyer's market. For example, this chapter is about increasing manufacturing flexibility, but traditional measures don't address this issue at all. As mentioned earlier, they may even detract from flexibility. Their fragmentation of the business, with the idea each piece should try to improve its performance in isolation, ignores the idea that teamwork is the key to success.

Look out, not in

Excellent internal performance is the goal in a seller's market. After all, you have no problem getting and keeping customers. In a buyer's market, it is excellent *external* performance that is key. So your primary measures should tell you how your customers view your performance. Sad to say, few companies do this well. Most fall back to the comfortable, traditional and precise ways of measuring internal performance.

It is not easy to measure external performance. For example, how do you measure flexibility? No one indicator can do the job so a composite of factors must be measured and flexibility then inferred. A reduction in set-up times could infer improved flexibility. A reduction in throughput (P) times also suggests improved flexibility. Determining how fast you could increase, *and sustain*, output 10% above your current production rate, then 20%, 30%, etc, is another way of looking at flexibility.

The key is to start developing your external measures. It will take time to get consistent data and to get comfortable with these new performance indicators. Ensure traditional measures of internal performance take a back seat to these new measures. These new measures will focus the whole company, not only on improving its external performance, but also on ways to motivate better team dynamics to meet clearly articulated business goals.

5

Getting designers to design products to maximize return on assets

Product designers are suddenly under new types of pressure. They have been hit with the 'design fors'. People want them to: *design for reliability, design for quality, design for manufacture* and *design for assembly*. Some companies have rolled these concepts into one and called it: *design for excellence*. And now here I come, asking designers to: *design to maximize ROA*. This requirement can be further subdivided into: *design to profitably delight customers*, hence increase the return, and: *design to minimize inventories and capital equipment*, hence reduce the assets. This double hit on the ROA equation can significantly improve a company's financial results.

I am focusing this discussion on design engineers, but it really is a joint focus on designers, plus sales and marketing, and especially product managers. These latter two groups influence dramatically the way designers design products. Only when all these groups work together can products be designed to maximize ROA.

Today's differentiation attributes

What motivates customers to buy one company's product versus another has changed significantly over the past 15 years. At one time, the physical properties of the product were dominant. Such things as performance and feature availability were the deciding factors. Then along came quality and reliability to add to the decision equation. Most recently, other factors have crept in, such as availability when desired, ease of ordering, problem resolution, payment options and so on.

These changes are shown in Fig. 5.1. Product characteristics are shown on the far left. The other three columns show the inclusion of other buying attributes. These changed buying requirements have drastically changed the balance customers want between the product and what I will call service, the other items on Fig. 5.1. As mentioned earlier, the proverb, 'Build a

Physical product	Pre sale support	Availability	After sales Support
Features	Ease of ordering	In stock	Field service
Performance		Fast Delivery	Technical support
	Technical support		
Reliability		On time	
			Warranty policy
Quality		Complete	Service parts
			Accurate billing
			Payment terms

Fig. 5.1 Differentiation attributes.

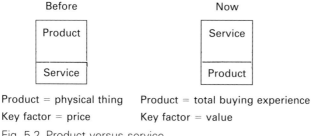

Before   Now

Product   Service

Service   Product

Product = physical thing   Product = total buying experience
Key factor = price   Key factor = value

Fig. 5.2 Product versus service.

better mousetrap and they will beat a path to your doorstep' has been almost universally destroyed.

This change can be seen in Fig. 5.2. On the left side, the product is dominant and service is a small factor. Today, shown on the right, it is the service elements that are dominant. There are so many 'me too' products on the market, with minor performance differences from the customer's perspective, that the service elements can become the deciding factors of which product to buy.

Few designers are designing with this new picture in mind. They are still working to develop that better mousetrap that only a few customers will really value. Instead, they should be designing products with adequate performance but with characteristics that allow the company to *wow* the customer with service.

A new look at designs

In Chapter 3, two of the solutions to the P:D ratio were, one, standardize the early phases of the 'P' time and, two, simplify the variety of end products. I will focus mainly on the first of these, standardization, in this chapter, leaving simplification of the end product variety to Chapter 6.

Standardization is not a popular word in the design community. Many designers feel it impinges on their creativity but, in reality, the opposite is true. You have to be a lot more creative to use standardized items to design a given product than if you have the complete universe of parts and raw materials to choose from.

Also, standardization does not mean a static list of choices. As technology or the product mix changes, then the standardized list must also change. The idea of standardization is to allow customer value creativity but to block unnecessary item proliferation the customer doesn't value. (Customer value creativity provides features that influence the customer to buy this product over any others. All other kinds of creativity are by definition, costly with little or no benefit.)

The real issue with standardization, though, is that products must routinely consider the market-place dynamics. If availability when desired, on-time delivery, complete shipments, no back orders and fast response are key issues influencing the customer's buying decision, then these factors must be part of the specifications for products. Meeting these requirements will almost always require standardization to be used.

Beware the non-recorded costs

When products are designed, many decisions are made that influence the final product cost, for instance, will the case be metal or plastic? If metal, will it be formed sheet metal or die cast? If plastic, what type of resin and method of molding will be specified? These decisions, and many more like them, will be made early in the design, with the choice normally based on performance and cost. The actual spending on the product will come later as tooling is procured and then full production starts up.

Figure 5.3 shows this idea conceptually. The left-hand axis is the percent of the product's life cycle costs that are spent. A product's life cycle costs are the total costs spent in all phases of the life cycle, from concept to product obsolescence.

The four phases on the horizontal axis show the normal progression of a new product from start to finish. In the concept phase, technical problems are worked out and proven, perhaps culminating in some working prototypes. During the design phase, these conceptual designs are defined and specified so the product can be manufactured. It may result in a pre-production run of product to iron out any remaining problems.

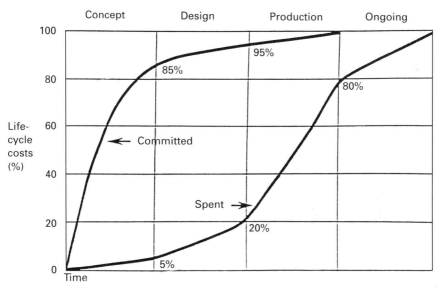

Fig. 5.3 Product lifecycle costs.

The production phase means exactly that, building and selling the product. It ends with obsolescence of this product, hopefully by being replaced with the next evolution. The last phase, ongoing, means the service of units in the field. Spare parts production and sales, plus installation in some cases, occurs during this time. But at some point even this phase of a product is stopped. Customers with these old units either continue to get service through a third party or are persuaded to buy the replacement product. One hundred percent of the life cycle costs means all costs expended on this product through these four phases.

The curve labelled 'spent' shows conceptually how costs are incurred on a cumulative basis. The percentage figures are for a high tech, short life cycle product. For many companies, making products without much risk of technical obsolescence, the percentages for the first two phases would be much lower. And for some companies, there is little or no requirement or opportunity for spares or service support. Hence the 80% figure at the end of production would be much closer to 100%.

The second curve, labelled 'committed', shows conceptually how the life cycle costs *will* be spent based on decisions made in each phase. As you can see, 85% of the life cycle costs will be spent based on the conceptual decisions mentioned earlier, such as make the case plastic or metal, sheet metal or die cast, and so on. By the time the design is complete with all dimensions, tolerances and specifications, fully 95% of the life cycle costs have been decided.

These costs we have been discussing are what I will call 'recorded' costs. In other words, these are the costs picked up and reported by the accounting system. But what about non-recorded costs? For instance, a product has been designed in such a way that giving good customer service is impossible. Back orders are routine and so are lost orders. Are lost orders a part of the recorded costs? No way. Few companies even track them well. But they are true (non-recorded) costs.

Another product has been designed so that you need huge inventories to give the necessary customer service. Is inventory a cost, picked up by accounting and allocated to the product that requires it? Again, no way. Inventory shows up on the balance sheet, not the profit or loss statement. Any costs of inventory are spread over all products, not isolated to the culprit products.

Still another product has been designed in such a way that it is very inflexible. You can't easily respond to market dynamics so you deliberately forego certain market-place opportunities. Is this a cost? You'd better believe it.

These three cost areas are all part of the non-recorded costs of a product design. Now, what if I change Fig. 5.3 so that the left axis is the percent of *non*-recorded costs. What will the curves look like? The answer is, identical. We design in poor service, high inventories and inflexibility.

How much could the non-recorded costs be? – in excess of the recorded costs for some very poorly designed products. One of the problems, of course, is that these non-recorded costs are difficult to identify and quantify. But they are real, make no mistake about that, and can be the difference between a product's success or failure.

The better mousetrap that failed

I am going to use an example, modified slightly from the actual case, to show the problems of designing solely for the left-hand column of Fig. 5.1. How the product should have been designed will be clear.

The product is a consumer electronics one, made in Europe, sold in Europe. Its performance is twice as good as the nearest competitor. The selling price is about the same as the competition. Its aesthetics were so good it won the Paris electronics show's award for the best new product that year. It received lots of free advertising in all the consumer electronics magazines extolling the excellence of the product.

Would you like a new product like this in your portfolio? Most will say; 'Yes please'. But so far I have only told you the good news. There is more news coming. The product is drawn conceptually in Fig. 5.4. There are 56 iterations of the finished product. Most of these are cosmetic, not technical differences. For example, is the color of the case – white, brown or black? What language is on the dials – English, French, German? and so on.

There are 22 technically different sub-assemblies. These are printed circuit boards after all components have been inserted, soldered, tested and burnt in. These 22 sub-assemblies can be manufactured from six bare boards. It's the selection of components and the addition of jumper wires that converts the six bare boards into the 22 technically different items.

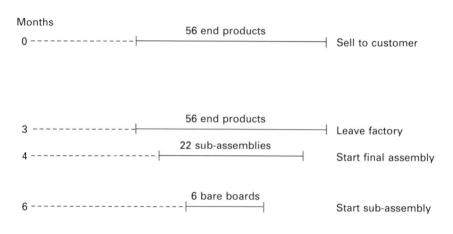

Fig. 5.4 Defining the 'mousetrap'.

Vertically on Fig. 5.4 is time in months, time when typically something happens to this product. Zero is when a consumer buys the product at the retail store. Three months earlier, that product, on average, left the factory gates. Why did it take three months to get to the customer? Because the company keeps one month's stock at the central warehouse. What does keeping one month's stock mean? It means, on average, every product goes into the warehouse and sits there for 30 days until it is picked and shipped!

The company has one month's stock in the main country warehouses – England, France, Germany, Italy, Spain, etc, two weeks in the retail stores and two weeks transportation time to travel between these various locations. Add them all up for an average of three months.

The final assembly takes one month. Hence at month four, the completed sub-assemblies start into final assembly. The sub-assemblies take two months on average to build, test, burn in and store ahead of final assembly. Hence the bare boards start into the sub-assembly build process on month six.

Some long lead time, custom made, integrated circuits have been specified for this product, custom made by a company in the Far East. The lead time to procure these application specific integrated circuits (ASICS) is 10 months. Hence they have to be ordered at month 16.

Variability at the last moment

I have a question for you. Look at the six bare boards in Fig. 5.4. When would *you* like to add the variability into these six bare boards to convert them into 22 specific sub-assemblies and finally into 56 end items? Most will say 'at the last moment'. The reasoning is obvious. The earlier you have to decide which ones to make, the more wrong you will be, giving you high inventories and poor service simultaneously.

When is the last moment? After the customer buys the product, of course. Let the customer add the variability. Is this possible? For some products the answer is 'yes'. As an example, built-in dishwashers used to be painted different colors at the factory. They never had the right ones in stock. A recent design innovation changes the front door to accept panels. Packaged in the box along with the dishwasher are several panels, one side white, the other black. Another panel is tan, the other side almond, and so on. The dishwasher is installed and then the customer selects whatever color he or she wants, simply by sliding the correct panel into the door.

As another example, GE used to offer lots of options on its mobile communications base station. They always had the wrong mix of options in stock. Now, all options are built into the unit. Customers simply select which ones they want through a set of toggle switches.

Software companies often deliver complete systems to customers on a floppy disk. Only certain elements of the software are accessible by the customer, based on the choices the customer selected and the amount paid. Additional elements can be accessed, simply by paying for them and receiving different access codes.

Beware the cost accounting system

Are all these ideas for adding variability at the last moment, good ones? It depends on the objectives. As mentioned earlier, there are recorded and non-recorded costs. So, if the designer's goal is to minimize the standard cost of the product, a recorded cost, then these ideas are all bad. Using panels to provide color on the built-in dishwasher is obviously a more costly design than painting the units different colors at the factory.

If the goal is to maximize the return on assets, then these ideas are excellent. For the dishwasher, there is only one end product, not multiples, so inventory levels can be reduced for the same level of customer service. Forecasting is simplified, only the total sales need be predicted. If you have any units in stock they have to be the right ones and, if the market-place suddenly moves to a rarely used color, it's a non-issue. The company can easily flex to this new demand.

Designers must design mushrooms

Returning to the European consumer electronics example, what if you daren't let the customer add the variability. Either it is technically too difficult or reliability or quality would be suspect.

It doesn't change the concept to add variability at the last possible moment. If you have to add the variability that converts the six bare boards into the 22 sub-assemblies during this manufacturing process, then the variability should be added as late as possible, preferably in the last production step. Again, if you have to add the finished goods variability in the factory, add it at the last moment. Lastly, if you have to have the ASICS to give you the functionality you are looking for, would you like one ASIC common to all the end products or would you like 22 different ones to provide the variability? The answer is obviously 'one'. You have to order these 16 months before the customer buys. You would have a reasonable chance of ordering the right amount with one, not a possible chance if there are 22 different ones.

This is shown diagrammatically in Fig. 5.5. I call this a 'mushroom' design. The stem of the mushroom is the standard items, purchased or made early in the manufacturing process. The cap of the mushroom shows adding variety at the last moment. Others call this a tree structure, the trunk of the tree signifying the standard items, the branches showing the variety. Use whichever analogy makes most sense to you. The key is to grasp the concept to add variety at the last moment.

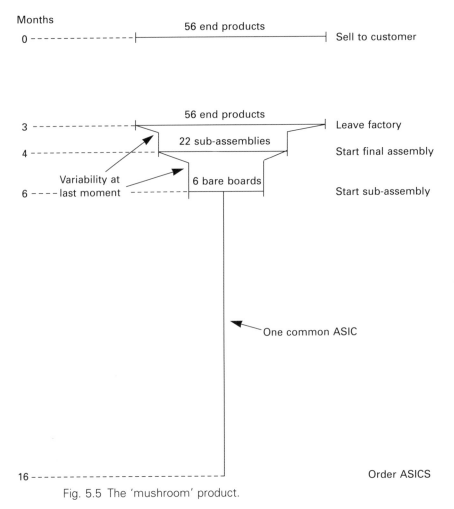

Fig. 5.5 The 'mushroom' product.

Recorded costs were dominant

I am now going to tell you how the the consumer electronics product was *actually* designed. The bare boards were made specific to the 22 finished boards at the first production step, six months prior to the customer buying. Who wants to volunteer to predict how many of 22 different things customers will buy in six months? I thought so, no takers!

Before I go on, please calculate when six months is from today. Does this make the problem clearer? Lead times alone don't have the same impact as the date at the end of the lead time. Please make this calculation any time you hear someone quote or talk about lead time. Challenge whether the date you have calculated makes sense. If not, you have to reduce the lead time or the variety or both.

The finished boards were made specific to the end product, again in the first final assembly step, four months from the customer purchase. Who wants to volunteer to predict how many of 56 end products customers will buy in four months? Same answer? Have you done the date calculation yet?

The long lead time ASICS were unique to the 22 boards. These 22 ASICS had to be ordered 16 months prior to the customer purchase. Figure 5.6 shows this design. Can you visualize the finished goods inventory? Huge and wrong. Dealers couldn't get the units that were selling while at the same time they had lots of the wrong ones. The factory couldn't react to make the right ones because of the inflexibility of the designed-in supply chain.

Six objectives for designers

Most designers have three goals and are measured on obtaining them. These are:

1   Functionality – does the product meet or exceed specifications?
2   Standard cost – does the product meet the target cost and gross margin?
3   Aesthetics – does the product appearance suit the application?

Under these guidelines, the example product was a winner. It had twice the functionality of the competition, met the same selling price, so we could infer it had about the same standard cost, and its aesthetics helped it win the Paris show medal.

But can you give good customer service with this design? No way. How about carry low inventories? Again, no way. And does the design allow you to flex quickly to the market-place? No way for the third time. These are

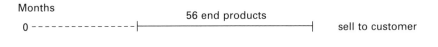

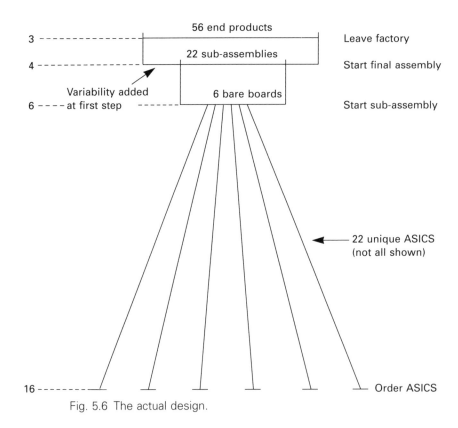

Fig. 5.6 The actual design.

all design issues. These defects cannot be solved by manufacturing, materials management, sales and marketing or accounting. They are in the foundation of the product, its specifications.

Three more objectives must be added on the designers' plate. These are:

1   Customer service – can you have the product available when the customer wants it?
2   Inventories – can you serve the customer with excellent availability with low assets?
3   Flexibility – can the production volume and mix quickly change to suit the market-place dynamics?

Hard costs versus soft benefits

I challenged the chief designer of the product shown in Fig. 5.6, why he designed the product with variability early in the process. His immediate reaction was; 'I have never considered these facets of my designs before. I don't draw pictures of designs like Fig. 5.6.' I then asked whether he had to have the long lead time ASICS to get the functionality he needed. His reply was astounding: 'No, in fact we built the prototypes from off-the-shelf components. We specified the ASICS because they were 20 cents per unit cheaper.' I then asked if he could have put the variability in later. He said: 'Sure, we could have specified plug in ASICS, not solder in. We could have soldered in a standard socket at the beginning of the process and simply plugged in the right ASICS as the last step. For the final assembly, we could have easily designed the color and language sensitivity so they could be added at the last moment.'

I then asked him why he hadn't designed the product this way. He said: 'First, nobody asked us to. Second, the standard cost would have been higher so we would not have met the gross margin requirement. Third, flexibility, service and inventories are soft benefits. They are difficult to quantify but standard costs can be calculated with precision. The accountants would never buy increased hard costs to get a soft benefit.' So a product that should have been a world beater, based on its functionality, price and aesthetics was a loser because of its inability to serve the customer, flex to demand and have low assets.

We will see later in this chapter how to avoid the hard costs, soft benefits argument. You can't win this fight. You have to build the customer service requirements into the market needs statement for the product.

Design, forecasting and standardization: the inseparable threesome

By now, you have some idea of the reasoning behind the need for standardization. It strikes at the heart of profitably delighting customers. I will take this idea a little further and show another company's approach to controlling design.

Comprehend the four forecast characteristics

Every company uses forecasts to make financial projections, plan resources and capacity, buy materials, make products and so on. The forecasts for these different uses can, and probably should be, different. They may come from the same base but differ in detail, unit of measure, time periods and frequency of updating.

All forecasts have certain characteristics. These are as follows:

1   Forecasts are almost always wrong. One wag once called forecasts either lucky or lousy. Faced with this, you must be prepared to change to suit the actual events as they occur, different from the forecast.

2   Forecasts should be three numbers. These are, best guess, the upper limit and the lower limit. You could even add probabilities of hitting these three numbers. If characteristic number one is true, number two must also be true. There is no one right number so define the potential range. The range tells you how much flexibility or contingency you must have to respond well to the actual facts.

3   Forecasts are more accurate for families. This is a mathematical truism, the larger the population you attempt to predict, the more accurate you will be. The more detailed you try to make the forecast, the more wrong it will be. This screams for commonality throughout the family – commonality of raw materials, purchased parts and production processes. It tells you to delay your decision on a specific action until the last possible moment.

4   Long-term forecasts are even more wrong. Again, a mathematical truism. An event forecasted close in will be more accurate than an event predicted way in the future. This is shown in Fig. 5.7 as the triple forecast error problem. Any time a manufacturer makes a forecast it is really three forecasts. It forecasts an item, a quantity of that item and the date

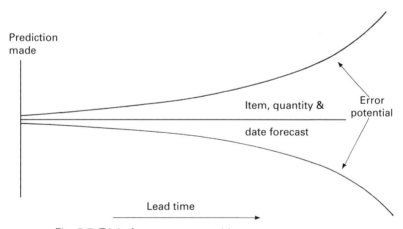

Fig. 5.7 Triple forecast error problem.

that quantity of that item is expected. The error in these three forecasts is shown by the trumpet shape, the error increasing sharply the further ahead of the event the forecast is made. This fact warns you to beware of long lead time items. They are what force you to predict long term.

Combine forecasting characteristic three and four to realize that, as you forecast further out, you should group products into larger and larger families. This grouping will help compensate for the increasing error over time. This idea is shown conceptually in Fig. 5.8. Time is shown as a moving scroll of information. Time winds up on the left scroll and becomes history. This is when the forecast is pretty accurate! Time unwinds from the right scroll so you always see a set horizon of the future.

Short range, you must be specific in both time and product definition, because you need to know the specific product to make and when, to satisfy customer needs. This is represented by the narrow lines on the time and product definition scales. It is obvious that the further in the future you push the detail, the more wrong it will be so broaden the time interval and broaden the product grouping to compensate for the error. At some point, this broader level of detail also contains too much error, so broaden both time and the product grouping again.

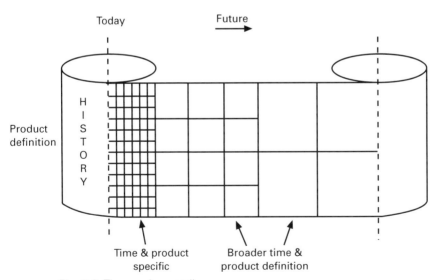

Fig. 5.8 The moving scroll.

A white goods company uses QME

One of my European clients, manufacturing 'white goods' – ranges, dryers, dishwashers, washing machines, refrigerators and freezers, uses the moving scroll idea to perfection. Far out, they require forecasts by quarter by large product family, such as described above. This is the 'Q' portion of the QME process. If anyone asks for a further breakdown, such as gas or electric ranges, for this far out zone, the marketing people tell them: 'We have numbers, but the numbers are all wrong.'

Some long lead-time raw materials and purchased parts must be ordered today to support sales in this far out period. Design engineering is forced to use standard raw materials and standard long lead-time purchased parts across each full family of products. The word 'forced' is their term, not mine. This is true even though, from a technical or performance standpoint, designers could specify cheaper raw materials or purchased parts for individual models within each family. They are forbidden to do this.

Is the reasoning clear? If they are allowed to specify cheaper items for some individual products, cheaper items that must be ordered today for a far out period's sales, they must get a forecast for the sales of the individual products for this far out period. We have already seen that specific item forecasts way out in the future are very wrong so we will buy the wrong amounts of these cheaper items, guaranteeing excess inventories and shortages simultaneously. This is *not* the way to design to maximize ROA! And now, will these cheaper items really be cheaper or will just the standard cost be lower?

At some point, some further definition of the product is necessary. This is the 'M' piece of the QME process – monthly breakdowns in more detail. This further breakdown of the product definition could be whether the ranges are gas or electric, the refrigerators side-by-side refrigerator freezers or chest-top type, and so on. This finer breakdown is necessary so they can procure or make the unique items for each grouping. But again, the designers are forced to specify purchased items and sub-assemblies that are standard for these sub-families.

The 'E' portion of the QME process stands for execution. This company's final assembly lead time is less than their customers' D time. So they assemble to order, from the standard sub-assemblies and purchased parts provided by the quarterly and monthly planning process. Their product availability to customer needs is outstanding. Their inventories to give this service are very low. Some carefully located safety stocks for standard raw materials and purchased items give them excellent flexibility to respond to market-place dynamics.

Design for ROA beats design for cost every time

The white goods company using QME has a competitor whose design strategy is to design for the lowest standard cost. Their designers have specified a huge array of raw materials and purchased parts to save a few cents per piece. Many of these lower cost items are unique to specific finished products or small groupings of products.

The result is high inventories, of the wrong things plus the safety stock manufacturing is forced to carry to try to give good service. Customer availability is poor because of the inevitable shortages. Expediting is rampant to try to make the bad plans they made fit the actual orders received. Actual costs are higher than the QME company which makes good plans and simply sets about executing them.

Develop your design guidelines

Designers have many procedures and policies that attempt to give them advice about how to design products. I want to add one more – giving advice how to design to maximize ROA. It is your choice whether these are guidelines or dictates. Don't forget the white goods company that *forces* adherence to the QME philosophy. These guidelines will cover the customer service and asset management side of the business. Measurements must be put in place to check that these guidelines are being followed or deviated from for good business reasons.

Expand the market needs statement

All new products get, or should get, a market needs statement. The target market, selling price, hence standard cost, performance requirements and so on of the needed product are defined. The traditional market needs statement needs to be fleshed out with the desired response to expected marketplace volatility. As mentioned earlier, it is a tough sell to add hard costs to a product for soft benefits. In fact, you will almost always lose this battle. So don't do it. Instead, build your requirements for customer service into the desired product specifications. Then there is no choice.

As an example, you have estimated that the market for this new product could fluctuate plus or minus 20% in total volume on a monthly basis. You require production to lag a maximum of two weeks behind this marketplace change. On top of this, you estimate that the desired product mix could fluctuate plus or minus 40% month to month. You require production to lag a maximum of one week behind this dynamic.

It is easy to see how these kinds of product specifications would block designs like Fig. 5.6. The length of the total supply chain stops this product from being volume flexible and the variety added early blocks it from being mix flexible. A quite different design would have evolved if there had been customer service specifications in the market needs statement, more like that in Fig. 5.5.

Ensure designers realize they have six objectives

As mentioned earlier, designers traditionally believe they have three goals. These are functionality, standard cost and aesthetics. Make sure your designers are also responsible for customer service, flexibility and inventories. Also, get them to think more broadly than standard cost. Move them closer to a total cost concern. Activity based costing (ABC) has shown that many overhead costs, either excluded from standard costs or spread evenly through arbitrary allocation bases, are linked to the complexity of the business. Reduce the complexity and you can take a swipe at overheads, the fastest growing cost for many companies today.

Design for variety without variety

There are two varieties, application variety and product variety. Designers confuse these two, often assuming they are the same. So for every new application variety they provide a new product. This guarantees high inventories and difficulty in flexing to the market-place dynamics. A better approach is to completely separate application variety from product variety. Now the goal must be to design multi-application products, similar to the built-in dishwasher example used earlier. Huge inventory reductions at the same time as you give outstanding customer service are now possible.

Control raw material and component selection

The need for standardization, especially of those things ordered at the beginning of the P time, should be clear. Create a preferred list of raw materials and components the designers are allowed to choose from. Don't let them deviate from this list unless their peers agree they cannot meet the product specifications by staying within the confines of the preferred list.

Items designed just for this company must be common across large families of products. If any items are required that are unique to a specific end product or small group of products, these unique items must have short lead times. Products which contain long lead-time unique items are doomed to failure in the market-place. You will never have the right amount of these so will not be able to profitably delight customers and still have low assets.

Design for short 'P' times

It's a rare designer who uses the lead time of an item as part of the item selection process. Technical and cost issues normally predominate. But the lead time to obtain an item is a key issue to the product's success. It is especially important if the item is on the critical path or it provides variability in the end product.

Every new product should follow a similar system to that shown in Fig. 5.4. This shows you the problems that you are likely to encounter in the market-place. Use it to drive the total P time down, to force standardization of the early parts of the P time and to drive down the lead time of the variety adding items.

Design 'mushrooms'

Variability at the last possible moment must be the watchword for designers. This variability could be of finished products, options, features, or any place where a choice has to be made to produce a different end item. Again, a diagram for the production of a product, similar to that shown in Fig. 5.6, can help you see how variability builds up in a product and give you ideas how to push the variability to a later stage, for an excellent increase in mix flexibility.

How to design products and get them quick-to-market

A study was made of the impact of various problems when designing a new product and their impact on the profitability of the new product over its full lifecycle. The study was of a high tech, short lifecycle product. The short lifecycle was determined by an upcoming technology shift completely outside this company's control. The study found the following three problems:

1   The development costs were exceeded by 50% (profit impact −3%).
2   The manufacturing costs were 9% over target (profit impact −15%).
3   The market introduction was six months late (profit impact −33%).

Figure 5.3 explains clearly why exceeding the development budget has little impact. The life cycle costs expended in the concept phase are only five percent of the total, so exceeding this by 50 percent gives the minus three percent profit hit.

Being six months late on a product when there is a stake in the ground set by a technology shift has huge profit impact. You lose six months of potential sales for a product that may have a life cycle of only 18 months. There goes a third of your potential profits.

This does not mean that designers should have a blank check for what they spend. Far from it. What it does mean is, if the choice is to stay on budget and be six months late or be on time and exceed the budget, it's obvious. Be on time. Beat up the designers afterwards about their poor estimating of the development costs but don't let budget control delay your launch date.

This example is for a high tech, short lifecycle product. Other products may not have the technological obsolescence issue to contend with. But for most products I believe this concept of being on time and over budget is a better choice than on budget and late. The penalty of being late to market will almost always exceed the cost overrun of the development budget. An even better choice, of course, is being on time, more quickly and on budget. We will see later some ideas to help you do this.

Four essential steps for a quick-to-market process

Few companies have a well thought out process to design and introduce new products. Responsibilities are fragmented, many people have new product introduction work added on top of a full work load and there is a somewhat less than professional approach to project management. No wonder many companies are too slow to reach the market.

Step one: adequate technological and market-place intelligence

Ideas for new products either come because some new technology opens up an opportunity or there is a void in the market-place which a new product could fill. All companies should therefore have good early warning systems telling them about these potential opportunities. Many companies do quite well at this, but then the problem starts. Much time is spent trying to nail down the exact specifics of the new product, what the market size might be, the selling price, costs and so on. These details are necessary before senior managers give the approval for a formal design effort.

This fuzzy front end cannot be determined with accuracy. Spending a lot of time trying to be specific about possible sales volumes, customer acceptance and so on, perhaps a year or more ahead of the first sale, is ridiculous. Not only that, but you are losing valuable time in your race to be quick to market. That is why step one requires 'adequate', not 'excellent', information. Excellent information does not exist. Trying to cross the 'Ts' and dot the 'Is' at this stage is a fruitless exercise.

If the new product looks promising, launch a design effort. You won't be spending much out-of-pocket. Create some milestones where you regularly re-evaluate the product based on the latest and best information. Be prepared to change quickly or cancel any program where the latest data suggests this product will not be a success. You will launch more new product programs quickly this way, weed out the bad ones later before significant out-of-pocket money has been spent, and give the good ones a head start to being very profitable.

Step two: a well defined new product introduction process and organization

As mentioned earlier, this is typically, 'Along with your regular duties, please be involved with this new product'. It should be obvious that anyone with these instructions will give priority to their regular duties. The new product is in the future, so can always be delayed. Today's urgent message requires immediate action.

The physical organization is also poor. People stay in their departments, perform their work on the new product, and then pass this information along to the next department for its input. This is called the 'over the wall' system of organization and is shown in Fig. 5.9. The development department works on the product, creates some preliminary specifications and proves the concept will work. It hands this data (the topmost arrows) to the design people who take the preliminary specifications and flesh them out in full detail. They hand this data to manufacturing who do its thing and down the line it goes.

The interesting thing is that the last people to get the information – vendors – are the first people on the critical path to make the product. They should get the information first to be quick-to-market.

There are six characteristics of the 'over-the-wall' design process. These are as follows:

1   Serial process – each department completes its part of the process before releasing it to the next.
2   Short development and design time – designers release a product and move on to the next.
3   Long total time – the serial process guarantees that the total time from concept to a product in the market-place will be long.

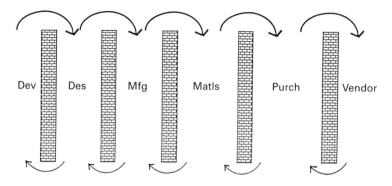

• Serial process
• Short design & dev time
• Business unfriendly products

• Many eng changes
• Long total time
• Low ROA results

Fig. 5.9 'Over-the-wall' design.

4   Many engineering changes – these are shown in Fig. 5.9 by the arrows moving from the right to the left. As each department receives information from the preceding one, it adds its expertise and finds that there are deficiencies. It now requests changes to satisfy its needs. This slows down the process even more and creates confusion and work for everyone. This is 100% NVAW.

5   Business unfriendly products – development and design people are specialists in the technical aspects of products and are rarely experts in all aspects of the business. Hence the design, although perhaps flawless technically, is deficient from many other aspects. It may be difficult to manufacture, have variability added too early, not be designed for quality and so on.

6   Low ROA results – these characteristics culminate in a product that does not profitably delight customers nor have low assets. Low ROA is guaranteed.

Concurrent engineering: a team-based approach

The over-the-wall design process can be likened to the functional layout shown in Fig. 4.1. Departments do a piece of the total and then pass it on. Responsibility and accountability for the total process reside in everyone, meaning no one.

Concurrent engineering says to bring together a team of people who have significant input to the total design, manufacturing and selling process. Get them to work together, like the cell structure of Fig. 4.2. Their role is to design a successful product and get it quick-to-market.

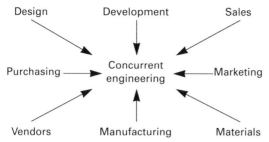

Fig. 5.10 A team-based approach to production.

This type of organization is shown in Fig. 5.10. A number of resources are shown. The arrows signify representation from those resources on the concurrent engineering team. I am not suggesting that every concurrent engineering team needs people from all these resources. This is just a conceptual idea. You could add customers, accounting, quality control, transportation and so on. The key is to define the critical resource input you need for a given new product.

Concurrent engineering defined

Many people say they are doing concurrent engineering, but on further analysis, they are not. Here is the true definition of concurrent engineering (deviate from this and you are not doing concurrent engineering): 'Concurrent engineering is performed by a team of people assigned full time to a project, co-located to facilitate communication, responsible for quickly designing a product that is a success in the market-place.'

Many so-called concurrent engineering teams have people assigned from different resources but they stay in their home departments. This is not concurrent engineering. Why co-located? Figure 5.11 explains the issue nicely. Concurrent engineering is all about frequent dialog among the team members. Separation inhibits discussion, proximity fosters it. Other so-called concurrent engineering teams assign people part time. This is also not concurrent engineering. Don't forget what was said earlier about what takes priority, your regular duties or the new product. If you are serious about becoming quick-to-market, you must be serious about devoting the resources.

Many people tell me they don't have enough resources to devote people full time to design projects. It has to be part time. I have a couple of answers to this. Firstly, maybe you have too many projects on the go at one time – reduce them to the high priority ones. This could free up the resources you need. We'll come back to this idea later.

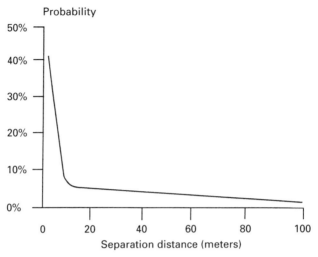

Fig. 5.11 Probability of communicating weekly.

Secondly, part time is a very ill-defined term. 'Devote 20% of your time on this new product' could mean 1.6 hours per day, one day per week, or four days per month. They are all 20%. Which is best? Full time for short bursts of time, so four days per month. Lay out the schedule for the new product. Identify the critical phases when you need heavy business oriented inputs. Pull the team together physically to work full time to define the business aspects of the product. After this, working part time on a routine basis for a little while for review and approval is adequate until the next need for full-time, dedicated effort.

What will be the result? – the reverse of the six characteristics of over-the-wall designs. Your success rate for successful new product introductions will take a huge leap upwards.

Get customers involved

There are two reasons to have customers as part of your design team. One, they provide expertise in the use of the product that you may not have. Boeing uses full-time, on site, customer representation from the big, world-wide airline companies. What do these reps contribute? Do you think there is much discussion about where the wings go? No, this is a technical issue and Boeing's engineers are quite capable of making this decision. But what about ease of maintenance? What about the ease of reconfiguring the inside from a freighter to a high density charter plane to a three class scheduled airline? What about the cockpit layout? These are items Boeing engineers know something about but they are not the experts. The people who do the maintenance, reconfigure the insides and sit in the cockpit are the experts. Boeing is clever enough to pull this expertise out of its customers for a more successful product.

Two, when customers get involved with designing a new product it will be difficult for them not to buy it. They become emotionally involved by being on the design team and through their ideas being incorporated into the design. You therefore increase the odds of success when customers contribute to your design effort.

Step three: standardized product modules

There are two ways to design a new product. Firstly, start with a clean sheet of paper and redesign the product from scratch. Secondly, reuse as much existing product designs as possible, designing only enough to make the product new. This latter approach is obviously best. It reduces risk, reduces the design effort, reduces the work for everyone else downstream and, more importantly, reduces the time to get into the market-place.

Designs should be a building block of standardized modules. This applies to software as well as hardware. It requires careful thinking about the functions of a design and how these can be segregated into modules. Once this is done, the effort afterwards is reduced for everyone.

Step four: skilled overall project co-ordination

New product design and introduction is a project. Most ongoing activities in manufacturing companies are processes. Process management is very different from project management.

Managing a project to stay on budget, meet deadlines and produce a successful product requires special skills. Select someone from the concurrent engineering team who has these skills and the time to be appointed project manager. Design engineers should almost never be project managers. In reality they often are. Why not? Because in most new product design efforts, the dominant work load is the technical portion of the design. Other functions contribute business expertise but not always with the same time demands as those on the design engineers. Hence someone other than the design engineer should be project manager.

I don't care which function the project manager comes from other than design engineering. What is important is the person must be trained in project management. Among the scope of activities are estimating resources, developing timetables – maybe expressed as critical path or program evaluation review technique (PERT) networks – and the timely reporting of progress against the plan. Deviations must be responded to immediately to get back on plan and meet the schedule.

Design twice as many successful products, quickly, with the same resources

I mentioned earlier, when I told you some people say they don't have enough resources to put people full time on a concurrent engineering project, that maybe they have too many projects. This was not really true. They have too many projects being worked on *simultaneously*.

Six ships tell a story

I am going to give you a riddle to solve. It should explain some concepts regarding focused versus diffused resources. Six ships are coming into dock to be unloaded. Six docks are open to receive these six ships. Six cranes are available to unload these six ships. I want to unload these ships and get them back out to sea as quickly as possible. While in the docks they cost me money, at sea they earn me money.

They are all going to arrive at the same minute of the same hour of the same day. That is called the law of random arrivals! They have been at sea for a long time so the sailors are anxious to get on shore. They will all dock at the same time. If I use one crane to unload one ship it will take six days to unload it. I can double up the number of cranes per ship (I only have six cranes) and the time will reduce in half. There is no conflict or synergy with multiple cranes. I can use three, four, five or six cranes per ship. The time to unload the ship is reduced proportionately. How should I allocate my cranes to the ships to reduce the total time in dock?

Take a moment to think about this. I get a variety of answers in my courses when I ask this question. Some say it makes no difference, others plump for one solution or the other.

I will do the calculation for you at the two extremes, one crane per ship and six cranes per ship. With one crane per ship all ships are in dock six days for a total of 36 dock days. The average time a ship is in dock is six days. With six cranes per ship, ship one is in dock one day, ship two two days and so on. The total dock days are 21. The average time a ship is in dock is three and a half days. Deploying the same resources correctly cuts the total time almost in half or the same resources could unload over 40% more ships.

Apply the ships analogy to new product design

You have six new products you want quick-to-market. You have six design engineers you could assign to these projects. What should you do with the six design engineers? Put them all on one project, of course. Drive this one project to a conclusion, then move on to the next.

This is the theoretically correct answer, however all designers may not have the requisite skills for every project. Too many people can get in each other's way. And, if your designers haven't worked in design teams before, there will be a lot of friction between the various people.

What the riddle *does* say, though, is to push towards a few, high priority projects with heavy, dedicated resources. These few projects should be supported by the resources of other specialities needed for the concurrent engineering process. The riddle further says never to let anyone push you into multiple projects all going at the same time. This is a sure route to disaster.

In fact, most companies behave even worse than one crane per ship. They give each engineer six projects to work on or each crane has six ships to unload! The cranes rotate between the various ships, unloading a little from each, then starting again. You can figure out the elapsed time this would take.

The reasoning for multiple projects per engineer is it fully utilizes the engineer's time. Utilizing your engineer's time is not the objective. Getting product quick-to-market is. When each engineer has multiple projects you guarantee slow to market and now your excuse that you don't have enough resources in other departments to do concurrent engineering is valid, but dead wrong.

Twice as many new products, half the technology lag

Employing the three requirements for quick-to-market – chop the fuzzy front end, use concurrent engineering and only work on a few, preferably one, high priority projects at a time – can cut the time to develop a new product in half. The same resources can develop twice as many successful new products. And, compared to other companies that are not using these ideas, you can have newer technology in the market-place way before the competition.

This is shown as Fig. 5.12. The solid bars represent the company using the three requirements for quick-to-market. The dashed line is a company using the traditional over-the-wall methods. The solid line company has many activities overlapping so can collapse the total time to market. Let's

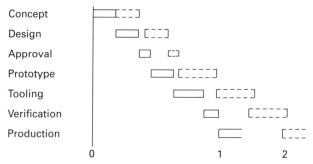

Fig. 5.12 Quick-to-market – twice as many new products, half the technology lag, half the invisible inventory.

assume this time is one year. The dashed line company, using traditional methods, takes two years to develop an equivalent product. They will be in the market one year later than the solid line company.

Look at the cash flow implications. All the development costs of a new product are invested prior to a sale. You don't recoup a penny of these costs until you start selling the product. I call these investments, invisible inventories. As I mentioned earlier, it is only a quirk of accounting that we book the physical, visible things bought prior to a sale into inventory, but other investments incurred prior to a sale, such as designing a new product, are expensed or, in some cases, capitalized.

The solid line company can recoup these invisible inventories much earlier. For many companies, their invisible inventories exceed their physical inventories. Speeding up the design to market cycle will have an enormous impact on their cash flow at the same time as they beat the competition with better products delivered earlier.

Use the six ships analogy everywhere

Some people are able to accomplish a lot more than others. They seem to do it effortlessly, not necessarily by working longer hours. They are obviously using the six ships idea in their day-to-day activities. They focus on one high priority item and get it done before moving on to the next. Most of us have multiple projects on the go at all times and bounce from one to the other.

Use the six ships idea everywhere. Any time you desire multiple projects to be completed, first prioritize the list, then focus your resources on the top item. Don't be tempted to work on more than one at a time. This will diffuse your resources.

The military have said for years to concentrate your firepower on a limited objective, secure it, then move on to the next. We in industry are guilty of scattering our firepower over multiple objectives and then wondering why we never seem to complete one quickly enough or to our satisfaction. It's all a question of focus.

6

Product variety, friend or foe?

Consumers and industry are being bombarded with more and more products. This additional variety may simply be different packaging variations, or it can be variations in options or features or it can be different products altogether.

The drivers for more variety are:

1 Customers, looking for some unique characteristic or performance which existing products do not have.
2 Sales and marketing people, trying to serve a wider customer base.
3 Design engineers, using newer technology to create a wider variety of products.

This increased variety has not been welcomed by everybody. In fact, there has been a backlash against too much variety by many groups. The large discount stores seem to offer a huge variety, and they do. But it is done through selectively offering the products that are the volume sellers of their suppliers. They 'cherry pick' each supplier's offerings to maximize return on shelf space or store square footage. They will special order the slow movers as a service to their customers but won't ever carry each supplier's full line. They are also brutal in their decisions about which products to delete. Any not meeting their profit objectives are eliminated in favor of more profitable ones.

Customers, too, are becoming confused by the huge variety of products. Go into any electronics discount house and look at the variety of VCRs or televisions on offer. Which one to choose? The sales people are rarely knowledgable enough to guide you to make the right decision.

The American automobile companies used to offer cars with each option as a customer selection. Today, many options are part of the base vehicle. Add-on options are often packaged into groups, such as a courtesy lighting group, where you get lights in the trunk, under the hood and on the doors. You can't get just a hood or trunk light anymore. It makes the option selection process simpler and clearer.

Manage your offerings to the optimum

Manufacturers have become more flexible over the past ten years. They can produce a wider variety more easily today compared to the past. But they cannot produce an infinite variety cost effectively. Manufacturers also find it more difficult than retailers to identify the winners and losers in their offerings. Even when losers are identified, manufacturers are not as quick to delete the losers, clinging to all kinds of clichés to avoid making this decision. The following are some favorites:

1   Increased volumes spread more fixed costs over more units of production, generating more profits for the business.
2   We have already invested in this product. That means from here on it is a cash cow.
3   Customers want a full line. We have to offer the losers to get the winners.

In certain conditions, each of these statements is true. For the majority of conditions, they are dead wrong hence most manufacturers have excess variety, way over the optimum. Their ROA suffers as a result.

The optimum depends on your objectives

I have mentioned the word 'optimum' a number of times in relation to product variety. There obviously has to be an optimum number of end products which will vary depending on your business objectives. If return on sales is your goal, then a certain number of products will be optimum. If return on assets is the yardstick, then a different product variety will be optimum. Market share would create a third optimum product variety. Earnings before interest and taxes (EBIT) creates a fourth optimum.

In each case there is an optimum. One product is probably not enough; infinity is obviously too many. (I hope all sales and marketing readers agree with this.) So the bounds of the problem are clear. What is the question you must answer? How many is the optimum to meet my business goals?

The optimum can be moved

I hope you agree with the concept of an optimum product variety. The specific level of this optimum can be influenced by a combination of several factors. As mentioned earlier, manufacturing can be made more flexible.

The concepts embodied in world class manufacturing (WCM), and described in Chapter 4, can permit a wider variety of products to be made cost effectively. The technology of controlling manufacturing, such as computer integrated manufacturing (CIM) can use software to make producing a wide variety of products easier. Designers can add variety at the last minute – the mushroom design, as discussed in Chapter 5 – again easing the problem of producing variety.

All these characteristics can move the optimum to a larger variety but they do not remove the concept of an optimum. All they do is influence its specific location.

Manage 80% of your business expenditures, 100% of your revenues and 70% of your assets

I have some tough questions for you. Why do you buy raw materials and purchased parts? One wag told me because he couldn't get them for free! Apart from that, the real reason is to make finished products. If you don't have an optimum number of end products, what raw materials and purchased parts are you buying? The wrong ones, of course, at least some percent will be wrong. Why do you hire people? These could be sales people, design engineers, materials people, manufacturing people and so on. The answer is to sell products, design products, schedule products, make products, etc. If you don't have an optimum number of end products, who are you hiring? Again, the wrong people, at least some percent will be wrong.

Why do you buy capital equipment? To make finished products is the answer. If you don't have an optimum number of end products, what capital equipment are you buying? The wrong machinery and tooling, of course.

Why do you initiate business improvement programs, such as just in time, total quality management, design for manufacture and assembly, activity based costing and so on? To improve your products and make them more competitive. But, if you don't have an optimum number of end products, the people addressing these improvement programs are wasting some percent of their time improving the wrong things.

Put this all together and what do you have? Eighty percent of your business expenses are a function of the product variety. All the purchased materials for production and most of the payroll are product related. The general manager's salary is probably not product related, nor is his secretary's, nor human resources, nor some parts of accounting, maintenance, etc, but the bulk of people are product related. Hence my estimate that 80% of your business expenditures are product related.

One hundred percent of your revenues come from selling products. This may not be completely true for some companies, earning income on their investments, from royalties or licensing agreements, etc, but it will be close to 100% for the majority.

Seventy percent of your assets are a function of your product variety. The inventories, capital equipment and tooling are all product related. The buildings and land are not, neither are intangibles such as goodwill.

If you accept my rough numbers that 80% of your business expenditures, 100% of your revenues and 70% of your assets are a function of your product variety, where do you think having an optimum product variety should be in your senior manager's list of priorities? Somewhere near the top, to be reviewed and managed regularly?

Where is it in fact? – not even on the list in most companies. It is a delegated and diffused responsibility. It is delegated to sales, marketing or design engineering. It is diffused among product managers responsible for different product lines or given to project engineers for specific product types. Rarely do senior managers look at the total offerings against the goal of having an optimum to meet their business objectives. When they do get involved with products it's to follow the schedule of a new product launch or to decide whether to start a design effort for a brand new product. This fragmentation of their interests is what causes most manufacturers to live with excess variety and a poor financial result as the consequence. This is not the way to profitably delight customers.

Separate conceptual understanding from actual decision making

Managing product variety to the optimum is a very complex process. There are so many issues that must be taken into account before you can decide to add or delete products. So I want to break this discussion into two pieces.

First, let's look at the problem from a conceptual basis and identify the pros and cons of variety. Don't attempt to jump to conclusions while this learning process is going on. Just evaluate whether the concepts are valid in the simple manner I will present them. I will cover the second piece, which is the conclusions that could be drawn from the concepts, in Chapter 7. There are many strategies a company could take, all valid under certain circumstances. Your job is to decide which strategy is best for your company or maybe for each product line.

Five curves tell a story

This next discussion might lead you to believe I am for or against product variety. Nothing could be further from the truth. For example, one of my clients, who produces ceiling tiles, used a variety strategy to expand his business. He designed unusual, eye-catching ceiling treatments for the public areas of hotels, office blocks and government buildings. If the architect or interior designer selected one of these products, the chances were this company could also sell him or her their plain vanilla products for the rest of the building. Here is an example where added variety really paid off in increased sales and more profits.

Another client, making process control valves, created so many unique products tied to specific applications or, in some cases, specific customers, that he ended up with a huge array of products. Niche players attacked segments of his range. He did not have the resources to defend himself against all these attacks so lost key portions of his business. Here is an example where added variety hurt the business, in both sales and profits.

What I am *for* is the management of your product offerings to the optimum. What I am *against* is allowing product variety to grow like Topsy, leading to a poor financial result and to periodic product rationalization programs. I want product variety constantly managed to the optimum, a critical role for every company's senior management.

The curves framework

The five curves will be drawn using three axes. The left-hand, vertical axis is labelled annual cumulative percent and will start at zero at the intersection with the horizontal axis. The right-hand, vertical axis is labelled in money terms. It is zero where it intersects with the horizontal axis and is positive above this point, negative below it.

The horizontal axis I have labelled variety. For now this will be end product variety. In Chapter 7 we will find that it could be a lot of different varieties. This data is organized with the highest selling product in money terms at the far left, the next highest next and so on until reaching the lowest seller at the far right. Most will recognize this as a Pareto or 80/20 distribution.

The sales curve

Curve 1 shown on Fig. 6.1 shows the annual sales on a cumulative basis coming from this variety, hence the curve will start at the left corner and,

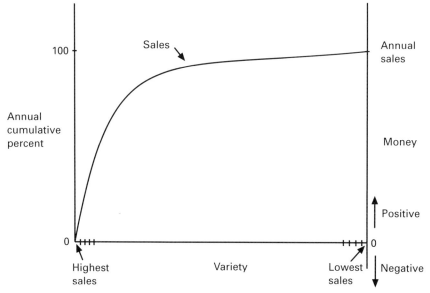

Fig. 6.1 The sales curves.

using percentages, end at 100% of the annual cumulative percent on the right axis. What shape will the curve take? Most will say a typical 80/20 curve, where 80% of the sales come from 20% of the product variety. However, this shape curve is not correct for the majority of companies. It is more frequently a 90/10 curve, where 90% of the sales come from 10%, or less, of the product variety. I heard of a recent analysis where 80% of sales came from 6% of the product variety.

Now, a quick reaction from you. If you are getting 90% of your sales from 10% or less of your products, do you have too many products, too few products, or do you think you are at the optimum? Most will say, and be correct, that you have too many products. It will be rare to find a company with this ratio of sales to products at the optimum to meet their goals.

This curve is in fact two curves. If I use the right-hand axis, money, then the curve is the same. All I have to do is write in the cumulative annual sales in money terms where the curve joins the right axis.

The support costs curve

Support costs is not a typical term in accounting or manufacturing, so let me define it. Support costs equal annual sales minus profits minus direct material and direct labor sent to a customer and retained as value added.

You can't subtract the material and labor used to make returned goods, scrap, obsolete and slow moving inventories, labor doing non-value-added-work, such as rework, changeovers, material handling and so on. You can only subtract what is value added to the customer. All other costs, what I have labelled 'support' costs, are spent, willingly or unwillingly, in support of getting the annual sales.

Included in support costs are all sales, marketing, design, accounting, purchasing and scheduling costs plus the materials bought but scrapped or made into obsolete inventories plus all the non-value-added-work expended by the direct labor.

Now to the curve. With no variety I would have no need for support costs, so this curve will also start at zero on the left-hand axis. It will also end at 100% (I am using the left-hand axis, percentages) on the far right axis. One hundred percent of your support costs have been spent in a year. What do you think the curve will look like?

Most people say the reverse of the sales curve. In other words, the high variety, low volume products consume a lot more support resources than the low variety, high volume products. Some may argue with this shape. But the best you could hope for is probably a straight line. Use this shape if you prefer it. It won't change the later discussion.

If I change from the left-hand axis to the right hand, then the curve will be the same shape but end at your annual support costs. These two curves, really one curve with different axes, are added in on Fig. 6.2.

The assets curve

Four different assets have to be added to get the total assets of the business. There are inventories; machinery, tooling and equipment; fixed assets of buildings and land; and accounts receivable. It's easier to discuss assets separately in these four categories. I'll roll them all together into one curve at the end to show the distribution of assets by product.

With no product variety you wouldn't need any inventories. So the inventory curve starts at the zero point on the left-hand axis. It ends at the 100% point (I am using percentages again) on the right axis. What does the curve that links these two points look like? – most say, similar to the support curve. The high variety, low volume products are the ones demanding lots of inventory. This is because of minimum quantities for raw materials, minimum production batches, erratic, unpredictable demand and so on. The low variety, high volume products need almost no inventory.

What about machinery, tooling and equipment? I am not asking why you bought it or how you justified it, but at a point in time you have an amount

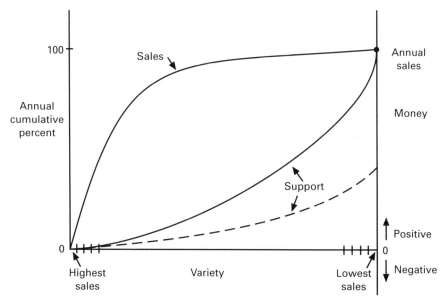

Fig. 6.2 The sales curves with the support cost curves added.

of money on the books classified as machinery, tooling and equipment. I want to know how this asset was used to produce last year's sales.

The curve will start at the zero point on the left x axis again. If you have no variety, you don't need machinery, tooling or equipment. It will end at the 100% point, at the right axis. What does this curve look like? – most say, similar to the sales curve but underneath it. High variety, low volume products have more changeovers, probably generate more scrap, more rework or reruns, and require unusual production or test equipment just for these products.

What about buildings and land? These are not truly product related but you could argue that you have buildings to keep the machinery and inventories dry and secure. So you could allocate this asset to the products based on the space they consume in production and storage. If the inventory curve is like the support costs curve and the machinery, tooling and equipment curve is like the sales curve, then you could say the buildings and land curve is a straight line from zero on the left axis to the 100% point on the right axis.

The last curve is accounts receivable. With no variety we have no sales hence no accounts receivable. So this curve also starts at the zero position on the left axis. It will end at the 100% point on the right axis. What does this curve look like? – most say, close to the sales curve. In reality, it doesn't look like the sales curve at all. Accounts receivable is a function of specific customers and our ability to deliver quality products on time, complete, with quality paperwork. Many times this curve looks like the support costs curve but I will assume it looks like the sales curve.

If I roll all four curves into one, the specific location will depend on the weighting of these four asset classes but, conceptually, it will look similar to the curves shown in Fig. 6.3. The second assets curve on the figure is the same shape as the first but uses the right-hand axis. It ends at your total assets as shown on your balance sheet.

I'll let you think about the three (six) curves shown on Fig. 6.3 some more. Do you agree they are conceptually valid? If not, change them to what you think they are in reality. Do not change them to what you wish they were – don't fool yourself with wishful thinking. I doubt your changes will influence the following discussion much.

The profit curve

I will extract information from the first three curves to draw the fourth curve, profit. It will start at the zero point on the left axis because with no variety, no sales, hence no profits. It will end on the right axis at last year's reported profits. (I'll be positive and assume your profits last year were positive.) This will be one curve, only expressed in money terms.

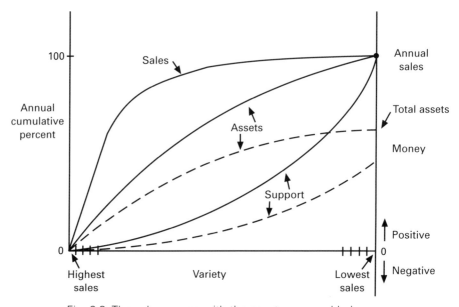

Fig. 6.3 The sales curves with the asset curves added.

I will take each product in turn and extract data from its unique points on the curves. The formula I will use is: for item number one, the far left item – profit equals sales (curve one) minus direct material and labor sent to a customer as value added, minus the support costs incurred on the number one product, (curve two). The curve of direct material and labor sent to a customer as value added is not shown. I will assume it is a curve with a shape similar to the sales curve. In other words, we send most material and value added labor to our customers with the high volume, low variety products. We send very little with the high variety, low volume products. I haven't drawn it because it makes the picture too confusing. Please visualize it, again as two curves, one using percentages like the sales curve, the other using money, ending at your annual, value added direct material and labor.

The profit earned from item number two is its incremental sales minus its incremental, value added, direct material and labor minus its incremental support costs. Add this profit to that from item number one. Repeat this process across the variety spectrum. A curve similar to that added in Fig. 6.4 will result. It shows that some products, those with low support costs, are profitable. The others, where support costs are increasing faster than sales, are obviously unprofitable. The net is your annual reported profits.

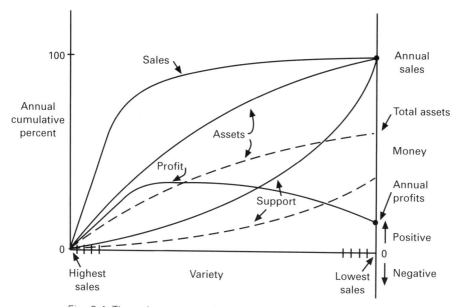

Fig. 6.4 The sales curves with the profit curve added.

'he return on assets curve

Today, you report one number, the return on assets for the business. This is simply the annual profit divided by the total assets and expressed as a percentage. It should be obvious that this is a cumulative number, the cumulation of return on assets for each product.

To show this, I will divide curve 4, profits, by curve 3, assets. The return on assets curve shown in Fig. 6.5, expressed only in percentages, will result. With zero variety, ROA is zero. Where the profit curve crosses the assets curve, ROA is 100%. Prior to this time, profits exceeded assets so ROA is over 100%. After this time, profits drop below assets so ROA reduces until you reach your end ROA result.

A reasonability test

Consider if you only offered those products that give you 80% of your sales. How many people would you need to run the business? How many assets would you need? What would your curves of support costs, assets, profitability and ROA look like? I am not suggesting this as your choice. It is *a* choice, one of many. I am just asking these questions to get you to check whether the curves are conceptually valid.

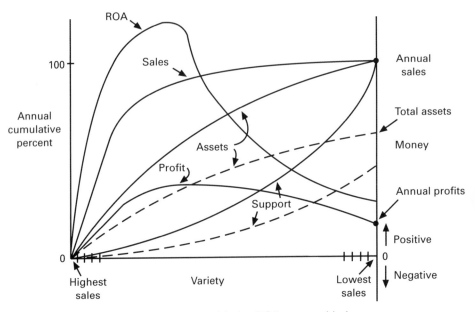

Fig. 6.5 The sales curves with the ROA curve added.

Is a zero start correct?

I have assumed all these curves start at zero on the left-hand axis, and increase or decrease smoothly. I am sure many of you disagree with that assumption. You feel that a lot of support costs and assets are fixed, so curves 2 and 3 should start somewhere above the zero point. But is this really true? Aren't all costs and assets variable in time? The best you can say is all costs and assets are semi-fixed or semi-variable.

The current business process re-engineering crusade has proven that a lot more costs are variable than we traditionally believed. In reality, very few costs or assets are truly fixed. One way of thinking is that, if my plant is not busy, I could bring in sub-contract work from other companies. In reality then, I have reduced the asset base for my products. The same is true for my support costs. Taking this to the extreme, if I only did sub-contract work, made no products of my own, then I would have zero assets and zero support costs for my products. Those I have are all allocated to other companies' products.

The trap of high fixed costs thinking

What's the danger of assuming high fixed costs and assets? You get trapped into feeling you have to keep a high level of activity to spread these costs over more units of production, even persuading yourself that low margin products contribute to paying for the overheads. You miss the fact that the increased variety of low margin products may generate overheads faster than revenues. Even more important, now you don't put anywhere near enough attention to reducing support costs and assets. This latter move will be a lot more profitable than spreading these costs over low margin products.

The curves are step functions

The curves are shown increasing or decreasing smoothly. In reality, some portion of the support and asset curves are step functions, meaning the profit and ROA curves are also step functions. Adding an overhead person causes a jump in the support costs curve. Buying a new piece of capital equipment or building a new plant also causes a step in the asset curve. These changes do not impact on the conceptual picture at all. They do show, though, why there is no direct link between added variety and increased support costs or assets. If there was a direct link, companies would manage their product offerings much better. But the point in time when you add products is decoupled from when you need assets or additional support people.

For example, the purchasing department finds it is having to buy a wider variety of components and raw materials. It absorbs some of this by efficiency improvements in the department and by everyone working a bit harder. But sooner or later, the increased workload causes a request for additional personnel. Why do they need additional people? – because they are buying more things. What caused this? – new products were added, with different parts and raw materials, several months ago. The full impact of the additional work load has now hit, requiring the added people.

This same scenario is true for almost all support functions, such as accounting, industrial engineering, scheduling, sales and marketing and so on. Each department gets additional work from added variety, some they can handle with internal improvements or just working longer hours. At some point the work is too much so the hiring begins. The cause, new products added months ago, is hidden by the passage of time.

Bringing capacity into the picture

What if I told you that 80% of your capacity is needed to make the first 20% of your products, 20% of your capacity is needed for the next 30% of products, and 10% capacity is consumed by the last 50% of your products?

As you can see, you are at 110% of capacity. What can you do? You say, I know, we must expand! We are out of capacity. So you invest in new machinery and equipment to increase capacity. But why are you doing this? – to make more losing products, of course, and to drive the ROA lower. I know, let's work overtime to raise the nominal capacity to handle the work! So now you pay a premium to people to ensure costs go up so we make even less profits.

I know, let's pay commission to our sales force based on the gross margins of the products they sell! Which products have higher margins, according to the accounting department? – the ones on the right side of Fig. 6.5, of course. So you sell the right-hand products as first priority, the middle products as second priority, and the left-hand side, low margin products as lowest priority. This will ensure you won't have enough capacity to fulfill all the demands for left-hand side products, guaranteeing lower profits.

I can assure you that the majority of managers in industry have made one or more of these stupid decisions several times over the past year. The pressure to satisfy all demands for products, regardless of whether they are profitable or not, is enormous.

Reserve capacity for profits

Capacity in the short term is relatively fixed. Demand from customers for your current product offerings is also relatively stable in the short term. What if your demand and capacity are equal, the demand made up of high profit products, zero profit products and losing products? What has to be your reaction if demand increases, from whatever source? The answer is to increase capacity. This is because, as just stated, the pressure to satisfy all customer demands is enormous. Deleting products from the line to free up capacity, the other choice, is a hard one to make. It also takes time to notify your customers and get them to accept your actions. After all, your sales people have spent time telling them how great your products are. How do you unsell them now without alienating your customer base?

A more sensible approach would be to use your capacity only for mostly high profit products. Only have zero profit products or losers for strategic reasons or because they are in the early stages of their life cycles. Reserve capacity so you can easily add promising new products or handle increasing demand for your existing products. Don't fill-up this reserve capacity with losers in the misguided belief that this is the way to make more money.

The 50% numbers are revealing

I will draw a vertical line at the 50% point on the variety axis and pick some numbers off the curves on Fig. 6.5. Here are the facts for most companies for the right-hand half of the product line: 50% of the products account for 5% of the sales, require 60% of the support costs and need 40% of the assets. I hope you agree that it will be hard to make money with these products with numbers like these. Finding out you subsidize some products with the profits of others is no surprise. All managers realize this relationship. Finding out which ones subsidize which others may not be so clear.

Thomas Johnson, co-author of *Relevance Lost*, says managers intuitively feel that 85% of their products are profitable and earn 110% of their annual profits. They give back 10% of the profits, subsidizing the remaining 15% of products. In reality, Johnson says, 25% of a company's products are profitable and earn 200% of your annual profits. You give back half your profits managing the next 75% of products. This relationship is approximately shown in Fig. 6.5.

As admonished earlier, don't take these comments as suggesting the only solution is to chop variety back to where profits peak. Subsidizing some products can be a very good business strategy. All I am trying to clarify is to what degree most companies carry excess losing products. The decisions to be made from this understanding will be described in Chapter 7.

Growth targets push variety up

Why does this condition exist so often? – because the major performance measure of sales and marketing people, and even general managers in some companies, is sales growth. Note I did not say profit growth, but sales growth. How do you increase sales? – by selling more of the same limited variety, a difficult job at best, but one that is almost bound to increase profits. Or ask for more products. Increased sales are now easy, but increased profits are often illusory.

Product line curves are often revealing

Many companies do a good job of analyzing their profits from product lines. They ensure they only have winning lines or good strategic reasons for the losers. It is within a product line that you often find the problem of too few winners, too many losers. Create the five curves, then, for each major product line. This makes the data gathering more complex to be sure, but the benefits will outweigh the additional effort.

The reason for this problem inside a product line is, as mentioned earlier, it is a diffused, delegated responsibility. Few companies do a good job of calculating profitability by product, so product managers and designers add products without realizing the impact on the financial performance of their line. It doesn't take long to get a product line to look like Fig. 6.5.

Cost accounting: help or hindrance?

Let me say up front, cost accounting people have come a long way in the past five years to recognize the limitations of traditional accounting methodology. Some very forward thinking people are turning accounting on its ear to provide pertinent information for managers to make good business decisions. However, accounting systems are so deeply embedded in companies that it will be a long time before these new thoughts show up as a change in the whole accounting process.

Will your cost accounting information mirror the picture shown in Fig. 6.5? I doubt it. The problem is the allocation of support costs to products. This is done poorly in most accounting systems, resulting in some very poor business decisions.

First, accounting splits support costs into two groups, overhead or burden and period or fixed costs. Overhead costs are typically costs related to the manufacturing process, such as the costs of the industrial engineering, production control and purchasing departments, rework, scrap, energy and so on. Period costs are costs not related to manufacturing the product, such as the costs of the accounting, sales, marketing and design engineering departments.

How are overhead costs distributed into product costs? – by using an arbitrary base, such as direct labor hours, machine hours, sales revenue and so on. The total overhead costs are divided by the base and a relationship calculated, usually expressed as a percent. The base hours or dollars are calculated during the standard cost rollup, and then the overhead is applied to get the factory costs. Margins are calculated as selling price less factory costs.

What this means is that the products that use most hours or sell most dollars, the fast moving, left hand-side products of Fig. 6.5, are charged with the majority of the factory portion of the support costs. The right-hand side products get very little allocation. This is in direct contrast to where the support costs were incurred, as shown by its curve. The right-hand side products incur the factory support costs, the left-hand side products get charged with them.

Period or fixed costs are not part of product costs. They are assumed to be independent of these costs. But don't sales people sell products? So shouldn't they be part of product costs? What about order entry? Don't these people enter orders for products? What about accounting? Aren't many of their functions, such as billing, accounts payable, product costing and so on related to working with products? So shouldn't they also be part of product costs? Putting these costs into period expense essentially says it costs the same for these activities if you sell $1 of left-hand or $1 of right-hand products. But this is not what curve 2 of Fig. 6.5 shows, neither is it reality.

'Peanut butter' spreading is dangerous

Spreading costs to products, using any of several allocation bases, usually results in high volume, simple products being charged with costs far in excess of what they incurred, with the low volume, complex products being charged far less than they incurred. This relationship is shown as Fig. 6.6.

The dashed line represents costing using traditional accounting allocation systems. The solid line shows actual incurred costs across this product spectrum. The result is high volume simple products are over costed by 10

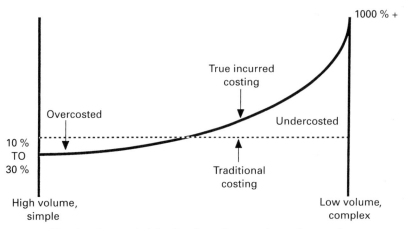

Fig. 6.6 Cost subsidization from 'peanut butter' spreading.

to 30% while the low volume, complex products are undercosted by 1000% or more.

These distorted costs become dangerous when used to calculate gross margins of the products. Gross margins are used to make all kinds of decisions, such as whether to keep or drop a product, where to produce that product, pricing, advertising and promotion, investment in the product and so on. Allocation systems will always tell you the left-hand products are low margin, the right-side products high margin. But margins calculated with this distorted set of data will have no relationship to which products are profitable and even less relationship to which ones are earning a high ROA.

How to quantify the curves

Before we explore this section, though, my first question is, 'Why?' Why do you want to spend the time and effort to quantify the exact location of each curve? If you agree the curves are conceptually valid, does it matter if they are one-eighth or one-quarter inch different to where you think they are? Will your decisions be affected by this level of precision? Aren't the decisions you will make strategic in nature, hence based on the concept, not the precision of tracing all costs to products?

For the majority of companies, buying into the concept will be adequate. But for the majority of companies you will spend the time and effort to prove to yourself the curves are valid, just to quieten the doubting Thomases. If it helps you avoid this waste of time, I can tell you all my clients who have created these curves tell me they are correct. In fact, the financial director of one of my clients, every time I visit this company, says, 'Your **** curves, they're right again!' As you will find out in Chapter 7, a lot of varieties follow the same pattern as product variety.

The sales curve

Developing curve 1 should be straightforward for most companies. Data exists in most company systems of the sales by product, either in units or money terms. Organize these into descending order for the horizontal axis, then create curve 1.

Three ways to quantify the support costs curve

The problem curve is curve 2. What data exists is distorted data from the accounting system. You will have to engineer this data yourself using one of three methods:

1 Judgment.
2 Survey.
3 Activity based costing (ABC).

Judgment

Break the products into groups that people can easily relate to. Make sure these groups conform to high volume, medium volume and low volume. Even two groups, such as standards and specials, can be enough. Now meet with the managers of each major support department. Get them to estimate how much of their departmental effort or costs are consumed by each group. Use these estimates to divide up the departmental budgets and charge costs to products. Make sure you cover both overhead and period expense departments to try to get the total incurred cost of manufacturing and delivering each product group to customers. Use this data to draw curve 2.

A judgment example: one of my clients makes process control valves. It makes standard, catalog valves plus specials. Specials are 'high margin' according to the accounting department, so a lot of sales effort is spent persuading customers that they ought to buy a unique valve for them.

The company used the judgment system to get at its true incurred costs. It found:

1 Industrial engineering people spent 18% of their time on the standard products, 82% on specials.

2   Purchasing people spent 50% of their time on standards. 50% on specials.

3   Order entry people (a period expense) spent 5% of their time on standards, 95% on specials.

4   All other departments were checked with a range of answers. In almost all cases, specials consumed over 50% of each department's time.

Now to sales – 95% of sales were standard products; 5% were specials. After curve 2 was drawn it became apparent that the high margin special products all lost money. The so-called low margin products were the real breadwinners.

Survey

Again, break the products up into groups people can relate to, making sure these are high volume, medium volume and low volume. Have all overhead and period expense people keep track, for a period of time such as a week or two, of where they spent their time, on which product groups. Use this data to prorate the departmental budgets back to products.

Activity based costing (ABC)

This is a technique that attempts to do a better job of distributing overhead costs to products. The assumption is that activities consume resources and products consume activities. Hence activities, such as purchasing, receiving, machine set-ups, shipping, and so on are each given a cost, based on departmental budgets and the frequency of that activity. Each product is then analyzed to see which and how many of these activities this product consumes. The result is a better distribution of overhead costs to products. This technique, because of the huge amount of detail needed to do a correct job, usually contains some approximations that diminish its accuracy. And few companies do a good job of tracing period costs to products.

The asset curve

Curve 3 is really four curves rolled into one as mentioned earlier. These are accounts receivable, inventories, capital equipment and tooling, and buildings and land. Accounts receivable is usually straightforward. Most companies' systems contain data on which products were sold to customers and haven't been paid for yet. This data can be sorted into the outstanding receivables for each product and then put into descending order to create its curve.

Inventories can be easy or difficult, depending on the level of detail in a company's system. If your raw materials and purchased parts are coded to which products need them, then simply summing all inventories under each product code will get you most of the way. Items common across several products will need to be allocated to specific products based on judgment.

If you don't have this product coding, then finished goods only will be straightforward. Analyze those ingredients with large dollar inventories and, using judgment, allocate these to the end products. Let the 80/20 rule work for you here to minimize the amount of detail needed. Create the inventory curve from this data.

Capital equipment and tooling is usually quite easy. Use historical records of items produced and the time they took on each major resource. If you don't have these records, use forecast sales for each product. Extend this data through each product's bills of materials and then routings to calculate the standard hours needed by major piece of equipment to produce this volume of this item. Use these hours to divide up the capital equipment and tooling asset base to each product.

The fixed assets of plant and land can either be bypassed, assuming they are not product dependent, or allocated based on the value of inventories and capital equipment each product needs. The assumption with this latter approach is that buildings are used to house machinery and inventories, hence allocating them to products based on the combination of these two assets can't be far wrong.

Regular reporting is critical

The problem with product variety is it always grows. As you'll see in Chapter 7, I'll suggest a regular process to continuously manage variety to the optimum. As a start, regularly report these curves, at least the sales one. This could be done monthly – as a minimum, do it quarterly. (I wouldn't bother with the support and asset curves this often, perhaps do them annually.) This data should be a routine part of the senior manager's information stream. It will set your company up to start making some critical decisions.

Be prepared for some surprises

Many companies are really shaken by the shape of their sales curve. Few realize how small a number of products make up the bulk of their sales.

Fewer still realize that many products just don't sell at all. The 100% sales figure is reached at less than 100% of the products.

Support costs are inexorable

Does the fact that zero sales occur for a product mean that it demands zero support costs? – no way. Sales people have to be trained on the features of this product, inventories procured in case of a sale, bills of materials and routings created, standard costs and prices calculated, upgrades or fixes to other products in the same family have to consider this product also, and so on. Sales can be zero but support costs keep on growing.

There is no way to avoid designing some low or zero sales products. The future is not that predictable. But, as we'll see in Chapter 7, many examples exist where the proportion of low and zero sales products is excessive, with a heavy burden being carried by those products that are selling.

7

Choosing how to manage variety better

The preceding chapter talked about the pros and cons of product variety. It attempted to convert an emotional subject for many people, product line management, into a logical discussion. As mentioned in Chapter 6, product variety cannot be reduced to a mathematical process. The mathematics, such as they were, were introduced simply to heighten understanding, not dictate decision making.

The key concept is, there has to be an optimum range of products to profitably delight your customers or meet any other business objective. Failure to manage to the optimum will cost you profits and assets, resulting in a lower ROA for the business. Be careful in thinking that the optimum for your business is where the profit or ROA curves peak. This may be true but other scenarios could be just as good, if not better, for your long-term business health.

Nine choices to manage product variety better

I have come up with a list of choices to resolve a product variety picture similar to Fig. 6.5. I am making the assumption that your picture is like this figure, a true assumption for the majority of businesses. The nine choices are as follows:

1   Do nothing.
2   Price to recover your incurred costs.
3   Chop variety and support costs.
4   Redesign: variety without variety.
5   Restructure the business.
6   Move specials to standard products.
7   Buy and resell.
8   Partner.
9   Attack support costs.

Do nothing

This could be a cop-out decision, letting emotion rule, or could be a valid business decision. How do you decide if you are copping out or being smart? List the few reasons when doing nothing would be valid and check if these apply to your company.

Four good reasons for doing nothing

Note, I call these 'good' reasons for doing nothing. 'Good' in this context means beneficial to the business in total.

1   Excellent financial results

If your company is enjoying excellent financial numbers, why rock the boat? Of course, the age old question is: 'How much better could we do?' And will we be able to sustain the excellent financial result as the curves slowly get worse, as they are bound to without a tight control on the product portfolio?

2   Linked sales are common

For some businesses, having a full range of products, the so-called 'one stop shop', is critical to getting sales. The knee-jerk reaction of all sales people when you suggest managing product variety better is normally, 'I must have the right side products to sell the left side products!' (The terms, left and right side products, relate to Fig. 6.5.)

Unquestionably, this is true for some businesses, but very few. Don't just accept this idea. Prove to yourself it is true or not. Analyze past sales and see how many times customers bought products from both the left and right side of Fig. 6.5. You will find, for 90% of industry, there is no link at all or it is inconsequential. A different category of customers buys the high volume, low variety products than buys the low volume, high variety products.

Even if you find the same customers are buying products from the left and right side of Fig. 6.5, this doesn't mean the sales are linked. (Linked means that if you didn't have the right side products they wouldn't buy the left side). Further analysis will be required, talking with your customers, to see how much they value a full range or would they be happy buying the left side products from you and going elsewhere for the right side.

3   Right side products are tomorrow's future

It is obvious, when new products are launched, that they will be on the right side of Fig. 6.5. They are in their early growth phase so need to be subsidized as they move to the left. Beware of the trap that products, launched with great expectations several years ago, are still on the right side. 'One of these days they'll be a great hit.' Don't let this emotional tie to products cause you to make faulty decisions.

4   Right side products are defensive

Sometimes it makes sense to produce losing products just to stop a competitor from entering your markets. The concern is that if they get a toe hold in your market by producing specialty products, they will be able to move into your volume business in time. The question is, how much profit and ROA are you willing to sacrifice to exclude this potential competitor? The curves tell you this, at least in general terms. You can now value this defensive strategy to ensure it is the best way of running the business or pick a different strategy to beat the competition.

Also realize it makes you vulnerable to niche competitors focused on your left side products. You have to have inflated prices for these to be able to subsidize the right side products. A niche player could undercut your prices considerably and still make a good return without the burden of the right side products.

Successful niche players are the ultimate test

If you have some very good niche competitors eating away at segments of your business, this tells you that you don't bring strength to the market-place with a full line. If a full line is deemed essential by customers, niche players cannot compete.

Analyze your competitors and their offerings. Find out their financial performance if you can. If you find that full line companies are dominant, stay with the full line strategy. If niche players are dominant, rethink your strategy. Focus on what your shareholders are paying you for, the *profitable* portion of delighting your customers.

Price to recover your incurred costs

Prices, especially in consumer or commodity markets, are largely set by the market-place, hence your ability to unilaterally increase prices is limited.

For many industrial products, there is a lot of latitude in establishing product selling prices. This is because an exact duplicate of your product may not exist in the marketplace. Customers' costs of switching away from your product are high because of the redesign effort that may be required.

The curves tell you that you should reduce prices on the left side products of Fig. 6.5 and increase the right side. What this does in essence is straighten out the sales curve. You are moving the slope of the sales curve closer to the slope of the support costs curve. This means profits will not decay from the peak but plateau at that peak or perhaps continue to increase.

Three reactions to price increases

As mentioned earlier, you could reduce prices on the left-hand side products and increase them on the right-hand side. I will focus only on the increase in prices as reducing them is an option you might not take. Customers could respond to price increases in three ways:

1   Acceptance.
2   Rejection of some products.
3   Total rejection.

Acceptance
Customers accept this change and continue to buy at their past rates. Some examples have been published where margins were increased 300% on the low volume, high variety products. The customers accepted these price increases with hardly a murmur. It makes you wonder whether your customers know more about your true costs than you do! It might also say that customers are willing to pay much more for specials than you thought.

Rejection of some products
Customers stop buying the right-hand side products, the ones on which you increased prices, but continue to buy the left-hand side ones. In this case, market forces are truncating the line for you. Don't forget to slash the support costs and downsize the business in concert with the product sales reduction. If you retain the same support costs and assets, you'll make less money and earn a lower ROA, not the best solution to the problem.

Total rejection
Customers are upset about the price increases so won't buy the left or right-hand side products. They want to buy a full line but your price increases

have made you non-competitive. The risk of outright rejection is what prevents many companies from adopting a more aggressive pricing strategy. You can try it out on a limited product line or slowly rearrange the pricing over several years. This will allow you to back off if you sense that complete rejection may occur.

Also realize that price increases that are accepted in the market-place have an enormous and immediate impact on your profitability. Some companies deliberately push the envelope of pricing as a strategy to maximize their ROA. They do this even though they may lose some business. This makes sense if the value of the price increase outweighs the loss of business.

Chop variety and support costs

I hope by now you agree that variety causes support costs. Low volume, high variety rarely contains enough gross margin to pay for its increased support costs, so the increased costs reduce the overall profit. In some cases, the increased support costs cause a company to actually lose money.

With this latter condition, losing money, you are more likely to take drastic action. This is what turnaround managers who are brought in to rescue a losing company do. They understand the 80/20 rule implicitly. They slash the product range, weeding out the losers, lay off a large portion of the support staff and can quickly return a failing company to profitability.

The White–Westinghouse story

In 1975, Westinghouse sold its white goods division to White Consolidated, Cleveland, Ohio. Westinghouse had lost money in this division for several years, even though they had invested heavily in equipment and managerial talent.

Three months after the sale, White–Westinghouse reported profits. Their approximate findings were: 20% of the product line accounted for 78% of the sales. Their estimate was that 46% of the support costs were necessary to manage the 80% of the products that accounted for only 22% of sales. They dropped the slow movers and slashed the support costs. It is easy to see how they quickly became profitable.

To complete the story, White had other brands of white goods that could fill in the gaps they created in the Westinghouse line. As long as retailers were not brand conscious, White could offer a complete line to their customers. Why didn't Westinghouse take this solution and convert a losing division into a winner? I am sure there are several reasons, believing they had to offer a full line is one. A reticence to slay sacred cows, products with emotional ties to some senior managers, is another. A third could be resistance to the social issues linked to downsizing the business. Whatever the reasons, persisting in losing money was a sure road to disaster and could have been so easily avoided.

A European example

One of my clients in Holland had sales of $30 million in 1994. The company broke even that year. The following year, sales were $22 million. It made $3 million profit! It found that a lot of its sales in 1994 were of special products in low volumes to selected customers. These had come about because individual customer requests for something different were passed easily through the technical department and then launched into manufacturing. No one realized the impact that all these individual requests had on the business in total. The company pulled back to its core products in 1995 and reduced support staff accordingly. The results speak for themselves.

Customers want to increase their profitability

Customers are creative people, especially with industrial products, and they are always looking for something a little different. This is positive for suppliers in many respects, such as freezing out the competition if you are the only one making this product, leading you to develop new commercial technology, and so on. But never forget that your customers are not interested in *your* profitability. They want you to delight them with something unique that helps *their* business. Your job is to make sure you delight those customers who will help *your* business and to walk away from business that will hurt your financial results.

Beware of market share goals

Many companies give objectives to their sales departments in terms of percentage growth in sales or in market share growth terms, but increased market share is only beneficial if, sooner or later, you can convert it into an improved financial result for the business. These improved financials could come about because your increased volumes give you economies of scale, hence lower costs, or they could come about because, with more market-place clout, you can now set pricing levels that give you good margins.

What does this say about market share objectives? – they can only be short term. At some point you must switch to enhancing your ROA. Dr J. Scott Armstrong, associate professor of marketing at The Wharton School, Philadelphia, analyze the long-term business strategies of 20 major corporations. Those firms that focused on 'beating our competition' or 'gaining market share' earned substantially lower profits over the 40 years analyzed. Dr Armstrong says: 'Maybe you should worry about increasing profits instead'.

Redesign: variety without variety

Chapter 5 talked a lot about the design issue. It stressed standardization, the mushroom concept, and multi-application products. This is what is meant with variety without variety. What you would like is application variety without product variety. Customers want application variety, you don't want product variety. It is product variety that costs you support costs.

However, as mentioned in Chapter 5, this means a dramatic change for the design, sales and marketing people. They must sever their mental links between application variety and product variety. They must consider several application varieties at one time. The objective will be one product that handles all the applications or a mushroom design that allows the product specific to an application to be produced at the last minute from highly standardized components.

It is critical to get this changed design philosophy firmly in place as quickly as possible. Customers can be very demanding for their unique products. Maybe you sold each account on the benefits of uniqueness for them, believing that customer specific products give you a competitive edge, and, in some cases, they do. Unfortunately they come with a huge support cost penalty.

Unselling these customers is going to take time. The sooner you get started, the better. Be prepared to lose some customers. Trade off the lost sales against a much lower support cost. If, however, you can successfully move customers from application specific to multi-application products, you have achieved a win/win situation. The customer gets a product that does what their application needs and you get a few products to manage.

Restructure the business

A high volume, low variety business is a completely different business to a low volume, high variety business. Mix these in the same facility with the same people running both businesses and one business will subsidize the other. It will be very difficult to figure out which is which. Allocating people's time between both businesses, even though I explained how to do this in Chapter 6, is not easy.

A better approach is to split the businesses apart. Preferably put them in separate buildings, each of them staffed with the minimum personnel necessary for that business. Make sure that the controls you put in place are also what is needed for that particular business. Do this even though you may have to duplicate some assets to have the two businesses completely autonomous.

If you cannot split them completely, for example the sales people sell both types of products to the same customers, then split as much as possible. Eliminate responsibilities that overlap both businesses. This way you'll be able to staff the two organizations with the right number and type of person that fits that business style.

Organizations grow to handle size and complexity. Many people feel the major driver of an expanding organization is business size. This is not true. Certainly, size has some impact on the organization. Span of control issues dictate some increase of an organization as size increases.

Of much greater impact on the organization size is business complexity. As you ask people to cope with more and more different issues, specialty groups spring up to handle segments of the business. These groups spawn more upper level managers, so hierarchy is born.

Mix complexity and size together and the organization really starts to grow. More to the point, rigid procedures are devised to ensure the business stays in control. These procedures may be valid for one of the two business types, high volume, low variety or low volume, high variety, but will rarely be valid for both. This encumbers one of the businesses with excessive support needs, guaranteeing one business will subsidize the other. In other words, the profits of the two businesses will be subtractive. One will make money, the other will lose money.

This is why separating the two businesses is so important. Set up your high volume, low variety business. It will require a minimum staff to operate as it is a simple business. Controls must emphasize the volume aspects of keeping the process running. Now set up the low volume, high variety business. It will require a multifaceted staff – everyone will wear several hats. Controls must emphasize flexibility and speed.

This should also require a small staff as it doesn't have size to worry about.

For the first time, you'll know the true costs of running each type of business. Now try to make them both profitable so the profits are additive. If this is not possible and you wish to stay in the non-profitable segment, for whatever reason, at least you'll know to what degree you are hurting your financial results for this strategic decision.

A building products company example

A large manufacturer of ceiling tiles has two plants. One is its high volume, low variety plant. It is very profitable, even though the selling price of its products is very competitive. The other plant is its low volume, high variety plant, what it calls the cats and dogs facility. It has never made money, even though its products sell at a premium over its high volume products. The company is kept alive simply for strategic reasons – some customers want a little of the specialty products for the public areas of a hotel, office block or government building. They then will buy the large amount of 'plain vanilla' tiles for the other floors of the building. It is a linked sale.

As such it makes sense to keep both plants running. Combine these two plants into one larger plant, with all kinds of sharing of resources, and this company would be less profitable. The organization would quickly grow because of the blend of size and complexity.

Move specials to standard products

Many company sales departments behave like order takers rather than sales people. They quickly acquiesce to any customer request for something slightly different, even though the standard product would be quite satisfactory. They let their customers behave as if they know more about the product than they do, the manufacturer.

Sales people must become more proactive, showing customers how the standard product will suit their needs, be of higher quality and more readily available. These latter two characteristics are almost a certainty. Variety and quality are opposites; variety and availability are also opposites.

The 17 reds

One of my early clients makes timers for appliances, such as washing machines, dryers, etc. These timers have a pointer that indicates the timer position. The pointers vary in size from three-sixteenths of an inch long, one-eighth of an inch wide to three-eights of an inch long, a quarter inch wide. These pointers are invariably painted red. In fact, they are painted 17 different reds, each one to suit a different customer. Arrange these colors in shade sequence and it is almost impossible to tell one from the other. At the extremes, there is a difference. How did they get 17 reds? – because each customer's designers brought paint chips they wanted matched or the timer manufacturer showed them a paint chart and let them pick any one they wanted.

Put this into perspective. A washing machine is at least a couple of feet wide and high. The pointer is almost invisible from a distance. How could the exact shade of red make any different to the aesthetics the designer wanted to create? The timer company should have selected three shades of red, one at each extreme of the shade chart and one in the middle as its standard. Customers should have been sold on the standard shade nearest to their requirements. Instead, the timer company was burdened with the costs and delay of 17 paint changeovers, carrying all 17 shades of red in inventory and the problems of scheduling the paint line 17 times to suit timer production.

Buy and resell

You don't have to be a full line manufacturer to be a full line seller. If you manufacture a limited line it can be filled out with purchases from other manufacturers. You could buy the products you lose money on from competitors that also lose money on these products, but they don't know! I won't tell if you don't tell. Or maybe another company can make these products profitably, because their business is structured to make high variety, low volume products.

The problem with this idea is that manufacturing people are arrogant. They feel they can make anything as good as or better than the next person, and at the same or lesser cost. They also feel that keeping their equipment running makes money for the company and, as Fig. 6.5 clearly shows, this just ain't so. Not enough companies follow this process of manufacturing some portion of their line and buying the balance. In many cases, it is not even considered. The routine process of design and then manufacture internally is followed almost blindly.

I realize that there are reasons to manufacture only internally, such as protection of proprietary technology, either of product or process. This should be a strategic decision that is reviewed periodically. Hanging on to an outdated philosophy of making everything internally, even though you are producing losers, will hurt your financial results with little or no strategic benefit.

Partner

This could be considered an extension of buy and resell, the previous section, however it is different enough to require a separate listing. Some products need ancillary items or significant other products to be complete. An easy example is greenhouses. These may require blinds for protection from the summer sun, tiled floors, watering systems and so on. It is unlikely that the greenhouse manufacturer would produce all these items, and it may not want to buy and resell them.

It could partner with manufacturers of blinds, tiles, watering systems, etc. The partnering would consist of each company listing the other parties' items in their sales literature. The listing could be as simple as how to contact the other parties if the customer is interested or could be an order form where the customer can order all the items needed. In this latter case there must be a communication device to notify the other parties of the sale, perhaps even including scheduling information to co-ordinate the installation.

Attack support costs

Curve 2 of Fig. 6.5 shows that variety creates support costs. This is because of transactions. Transactions demand people and other resources. A transaction happens when data or material is gathered, procured, entered, recorded, sent somewhere, stored, inspected, moved, etc. The easy activities to see this phenomenon in action are stockrooms, warehouses and material handling. A transaction in the sales department is a customer call or visit, an order being placed, a price list being updated, sales personnel training and so on. A transaction in design engineering is an engineering change notice (ECN) being created and processed, a customer enquiry or complaint being researched, etc. All these transactions require or involve people and time. They become a large part of my term 'support costs'.

Many of the concepts coming out of the just in time (JIT), total quality management (TQM), business process re-engineering (BPR) and activity based costing (ABC) philosophies attack and reduce support costs. But there is a minimum attainable level of support costs, determined by the number of transactions and how they are handled.

What causes transactions? – variety of products, components, ingredients, options, features, etc, and, as you'll see later, the variety of many other business characteristics. How far can you reduce support costs? – down to a floor caused by the varieties mentioned above, plus your methods to handle the resultant transactions. Now your only choice left is to address the varieties.

The importance of addressing support costs cannot be stressed enough. As you lower curve 2 from Fig. 6.5 more products become profitable and overall company profitability increases. Use all the ideas from the philosophies mentioned earlier to reduce what could easily be called NVAW in the business.

Is this the real world?

I have referenced several companies already and their experiences in managing variety. Here are some more, taken from the business literature.

Excessive variety in automobiles

It was reported in the *Wall Street Journal*, 8 March 1993, that: 'A slump in car sales forces Nissan to start cutting swollen costs. Its wild growth in variations of models and designs is now being reversed.' The report goes on to say: 'The company's top designers have been ordered to renounce a nearly decade long quest to build cars in ever more sizes, colors and functions to satisfy the presumed whims of the world's drivers. That effort, Nissan now realizes, spun out of control.'

I would like to introduce a critical concept here called 'Customer valued creativity'. By this I mean something unique in a product that will influence the customer positively to buy this product. Hence the cost of adding and managing this unique thing could be easily paid for by increased sales. Other forms of creativity, designing unique things that have no impact on the buying decision, are obviously creativity for creativity's sake.

Let's tune in again to Nissan. 'In the current model line-up alone, Nissan offers 437 different kinds of dashboard meters (maybe you are into dashboard meters), 110 types of radiators (I am sure the design of a radiator really influences customers to buy), 1200 types of floor carpets and more than 300 varieties of ashtrays.'

'Nissan engineers recently discovered [I love that word. Out of the woodwork came. . . .] that 70 of the 87 types of steering wheels for the Laurel model alone accounted for just 5% of the total installed. Indeed, 50% of Nissan's model variations contributed only about 5% of total sales.' First of all, having 87 different types of steering wheels for one model car astounds me. The 70 contributing 5% of sales means their Pareto curve of sales is a 95/20 curve, 95% of sales come from 20% of the product line!

Now visualize the costs of the 70 steering wheels. Tooling, design, inventory, scheduling, spares support, instruction manuals, costing, billing and on it goes. Now visualize the benefits. How many customers bought cars because of this profusion of choices in steering wheels? Not many, as the 5% sales tells you, and most of those sales probably would have occurred anyway with fewer steering wheel choices. I certainly wouldn't categorize this variety as customer valued creativity.

Excessive variety in personal computers

One of my clients used to make personal computers (PCs). It was a money losing division of a large company, hence its interest in using my services. An analysis of its sales by product class is shown in Fig. 7.1. Column one lists the variety of product classes. A class is a grouping of models with common base features. Nine classes of PCs were offered. Column two lists the number of unique models in each class, for example, class 3220 consisted of 21 different end models. Column three shows how many of the models in each class were never ordered by customers, and this is 18 months after these products were launched, pretty much at the end of their life cycles! Column four shows how many models out of the total accounted for less than 5% of the total sales. Column four includes column three. Again, for class 3220, it contains 21 models of which 9 were never sold and 16 models accounted for less than 5% of the total ordered.

Look at the totals. Out of 196 models, 95 or 48% were never sold and 153 or 78% accounted for less than 5% of the total sales. Figure 7.2 shows the same picture for the features that were available to be added to these models. A similar condition emerges.

I realize when you launch a new product line you are never sure which products will sell – so some excessive product variety is unavoidable – but I don't believe this amount of excessive variety was necessary. What a waste of scarce design talent. I am sure they had to compromise on the designs

Class	# Models	# Models No orders	# Models <5% orders
3220	21	9	16
3225	8	3	4
3230	44	22	38
3321	14	5	10
3330	37	24	29
3331	5	0	1
3335	17	6	13
3345	19	9	17
3350	31	17	25
Total	196	95	153
% Total		48%	78%

Fig. 7.1 Model complexity.

Class	# Features	# Features No orders	# Features <5% orders
3220	15	4	4
3225	16	9	12
3230	22	7	13
3321	27	14	17
3330	25	8	14
3331	16	2	4
3335	26	7	14
3345	26	3	10
3350	34	12	20
Total	207	66	108
% Total		32%	52%

Fig. 7.2 Feature complexity.

to accept this much variety, probably at additional cost. And, on top of it all, all support groups had to add people to cope with this variety. No wonder they were a losing division. It was eventually shut down.

Make conscious choices

As stated in Chapter 6, product variety management is a delegated and diffused responsibility. For most companies, the portfolio of offerings are like Topsy – they just grew. You must sort through the choices I have described or create some more of your own. Now evaluate the pros and cons of each choice *vis à vis* your situation. No outsider can do this for you – detailed knowledge of your business and its competitive structure is necessary to wade through the various options and choose the best. Now create a product portfolio management process, described later, that embodies your choice. The objective now is managing your offerings always to the optimum for your business.

Control a variety of varieties

Figure 6.5 was drawn with the horizontal (x) axis end product variety, but these curves are just as applicable to a flock of other varieties. For example, the 'x' axis of Fig. 6.5 could be options or features that are added to the base product. The same picture as Fig. 6.5 will result.

Order sizes

How about order size? – the value of a customer order that is placed. One of my clients drew Fig. 6.5's curves with order size as the 'x' axis. He put large orders to the left, small orders to the right and quickly found that orders under a certain size all lost money. The costs of processing the order through his business exceeded the margin value of the order.

He decided the company was not a charitable concern – at least not by design. So out went directions to the sales force. 'If customers want to enter orders with less than a certain value, tell them, no. If they insist, charge them an up front fee for the privilege of entering the order.' This company's profits have increased rather dramatically.

Customers

It is obvious one customer is not enough, but infinity would be too many. There has to be an optimum number of customers to maximize your profitability.

One of my clients in Holland drew Fig. 6.5 with customers as the 'x' axis. Before this it was using gross margin as the driver of the sales effort. Accounting told them that small customers were higher margin than large customers because large customers demanded large price discounts. So the whole strategy of the sales force was to go after small customers.

After drawing Fig. 6.5, the company found that large customers were very profitable, small customers were marginally profitable or losers. The problem was the support costs necessary to take care of small customers. Of even more importance, the large customer segment was the growing portion of this business that it had deliberately been ignoring. It was losing market share at the same time it thought it was being profit conscious.

The company redirected the sales force, withdrew support from the small customer base and even refused to do business directly with some small customers. It suggested that small customers deal through their distributor network, a much more cost effective way of handling small customers. It is now back on track, with growing market share and profitability.

Miscellaneous

Figure 7.3 is a list of varieties that need to be controlled. I have covered some in detail. The issue is whether any of these varieties has the potential of gaining you increased revenues or only of increasing costs. As you can see, most can only increase costs, at least support costs, and, in most cases, these increased support costs will outweigh any direct savings.

Drive standardization as one of your primary cost reduction or cost avoidance tools. You'll need to put teeth in this program because it is always

- End products
- Options
- Raw materials/ingredients
- Components
- Customers
- Order sizes
- Processes
- Vendors
- Tooling
- Machinery
- Tolerances
- Finishes
- Etc

Fig. 7.3 Variety types.

easier to not conform to the standardization rules. Your total costs will reduce as a function of how aggressive you make this program.

Standardization control during design reviews

Design reviews and concurrent engineering were described in Chapter 5. Here is a good place to control most varieties. All those related to product, such as tooling, tolerances, finishes, processes, vendors and so on should be scrutinized to make sure that standardization rules are being adhered to. Force any deviations to be fully justified as being total cost savings or customer valued variation.

Five steps to manage your product offerings

The case for managing product variety is clear – 100% of revenues, 70% of assets and 80% of business expenses are a function of your offerings. This should put managing product variety near the top of senior managers' lists of things to do routinely.

Step one: understand variety costs/benefits

The curves of Fig. 6.5 can be quite dangerous. Please don't use them for decision making. Their role is to explain the problem of support costs and how they increase with variety. As mentioned in Chapter 6, support costs and assets increase in steps, not in a smooth curve. Decision making comes after you understand the curves and you have evaluated the nine choices explained earlier. Use the curves simply for understanding. Draw them for your business, at least the easy ones, if you think it is necessary to persuade the doubters that the curves are conceptually correct.

Step two: evaluate existing/proposed products

Every product in your line should have a specific reason to be there – most hopefully, because it is profitable. Others could be new products going through their introduction phase. Some could be strategically kept in the line to defend against competitors entering your markets. Still others will be determined to be losers with no valid business reason to keep.

Make sure every product is clearly identified with one of these labels. Don't accept vacillation or emotional reasons with no valid business backing. That is how you got into this mess to start with.

Step three: routinely prune losers

Adding products to your portfolio is an ongoing process. Customers ask for more, sales people want more, engineers design more, etc. There is no countervailing pressure for less, so product portfolios grow and grow. Sooner or later, everyone in the company realizes there are too many products. This is the time to launch a 'product rationalization program'. It occurs on a routine schedule about once in every five years in most companies.

A team is formed, of sales, design, manufacturing and accounting people to evaluate the offerings. It is given a goal of how many products to delete. Working from accounting data it analyzes profitability, customer buying habits etc, and decides what has to go. As often as not, it deletes profitable products rather than the losers because of the erroneous accounting information mentioned earlier. It rarely draws Fig. 6.5 to see which items are truly profitable and which are truly losers.

After it meets its goal for product reductions, the team is disbanded. The same day, a new product is added. The whole process repeats itself until five years go by and it is obvious to everyone the portfolio is excessive again. This is not management, it is mismanagement. You must create a regular pruning process, carried out quarterly as a minimum. Any less often than this you will find too many excuses not to do it at all. Each quarter, go through the evaluation process in step two, then call together the pruning committee which should consist as a minimum of the senior managers of sales, accounting, manufacturing and design engineering. Show them the results of step two and, if no objections are made, put the losers on an obsolete, phase out track.

Step four: develop new products with high success potential

This is a bit of a motherhood statement, but you will be able to determine, through your analysis in steps one to three, some of the characteristics of successful products and those that generally constitute failure. Successful in this context is earning a high ROA, not technically successful.

Some companies link together steps three and four. They force discussion of what products to delete before they consider any new additions. These actions are both done quarterly. In this way, senior managers can see what is happening to the total portfolio and can ensure it is kept to the optimum.

Step five: post audit new products

Ask for $1 million for a new piece of equipment in the plant. Immediately questions are raised about return on investment, discounted cash flow and so on. Documentation must be provided to prove this investment will be paid back. Multiple levels of management have to sign off on the investment.

After the equipment is installed, a formal post audit is conducted to see if the equipment is performing as predicted and if the rate of return is being met or exceeded. Senior managers regularly walk out on the plant floor to see if the equipment is running. Woe betide the plant manager who doesn't make the numbers.

Ask for $1 million for a new product development program. Questions will be raised about the sales volume, pricing, costing, etc of this new product. A form of justification will be done, but rarely with the same detail as equipment justification. The appeal of the new product and visions of increasing sales will take over.

The new product is eventually launched with much fanfare. Questions will be asked a few months later about the new product, but rarely as part of a formal process. If the numbers are not being met, shoulders will be shrugged and the excuse will be that there is always risk with any new product.

Why the bias? $1 million for equipment costs the same as $1 million for new products and the equipment is a better investment, even if it doesn't make the numbers, because you still have it. It can pay back over a longer term or even be sold. New products, if not accepted in the market-place, are just a lost cause.

Create a formal post audit process, 6 months, 12 months, maybe 18 months after every major product launch. Be as rigorous as with equipment post audits. The reason is not to point fingers at anyone but to learn what characteristics constitute a successful or failing product. Roll this learning back into the design process, step four. For the first time you will be cost justifying the expense of the design department.

One client, making carpets, introduced this process. It quickly found that many so-called new products were trivial differences from existing products. This was done to meet an arbitrary management goal that, '35% of our sales should be from products developed in the last 5 years'. The goal was met but at what cost? The styling department has since been cut by 50%. It had far too many people developing trivial differences that were not necessary.

Beware of customer backlash

When starting a product portfolio management process you must realize that customers have been spoilt in the past. They have become used to your excessive product variety. They may even have been sold on some unique products that are now candidates for deletion.

Don't have a major house cleaning at the start of the regular pruning process. Come up with a short list of the no-brainers you plan to delete. Circulate this list to your customers and wait for their reactions. If you get violent objection to any on the delete list, add them back to the products you'll keep for a while, at least now you have a specific reason to keep these products. Adding them back into your catalog will give you a lot of positive customer goodwill as well.

One quarter later, circulate the next list of no-brainers plus maybe some contentious products. Again, add back any that generate violent objections from customers. Keep doing this quarterly. You must train your customers to accept that, as new products are added, you need to delete others. These two actions are part and parcel of any product portfolio management process.

8

Don't flex the factory, stabilize the demand

Chapters 4 and 5 described how to make the business more flexible. Quick change-overs, cell layouts, continuous flow processes and mushroom designs are a few of the flexibility-enhancing techniques. But what if you have done everything you can think of to increase your flexibility but the market-place dynamics are still excessive? They exceed your new found flexibility by a significant margin.

Four choices to manage excessive market-place dynamics

Chapter 2 mentioned two of your choices when demand volatility exceeds your company's flexibility. In fact there are four choices.

Choice one: decouple demand and supply with inventory

Produce finished or semi-finished inventories ahead of the sale. Let this build-up of inventory buffer the excessively dynamic demand from the inadequate flexibility. The problem here, of course, is two-fold. One, your financial results will be impacted negatively. Two, how do you predict the right items to produce ahead of the sale? This is especially difficult with dynamic demand because dynamic demand is usually unpredictable. If you don't predict well you have the negative of poorer financial results without the benefit of accommodating the dynamic demand.

Choice two: decouple demand and supply with lead times

As demand grows, quote longer lead times to your customers. As it declines, quote shorter ones. But, as stated earlier, meeting your quoted lead times is not good customer service unless your quoted times meet your customers' wishes. Adjusting lead times to suit the dynamics of demand guarantees you will rarely meet your customers' wishes.

Choice three: focus on a restricted market segment

Analyze where your dynamic demand comes from. Serve only those segments of the market-place where the dynamics are less than your flexibility. Provided this restricted segment gives you adequate volume, you will be more profitable and will delight these customers with excellent service.

Choice four: address market-place dynamics: stabilize induced volatility

Market-place volatility comes from two distinctly different sources. First, there is the inherent underlying volatility, caused by seasonality, customer fads and so on. Second, there is an induced volatility, caused by our actions, policies and programs. At least, then, we should evaluate our actions to see what contribution they make to the total dynamics. Perhaps we are the biggest contributor. Changing our actions to create a more stable demand, one that fits within the business' flexibility, would be the best solution. We would be able to make our company look very similar to Fig. 2.5, the Utopian business.

What would you like your demand to be?

I ask this question routinely at the management seminars I conduct. I ask everyone to put on a business person's hat, not their functional hat. After a few moment's hesitation, the answers will be, 'stable', 'predictable'. I then ask what they would *not* like their demand to be? The answers are the reverse, of course – 'unstable', 'unpredictable'.

I then ask the $64,000 question: 'What policies, procedures, processes and actions are at work right now in your company that are trying to give you stable, predictable demand?' The answer is usually 'zero'. In reality it is worse than zero. Many actions in a company are designed to give unstable, unpredictable demand. These are the actions that I want to challenge. I will list some of the major ones. Your job is to identify your unique causes of dynamic demand and then come up with the correct solutions. Don't forget, the objective is stable, predictable demand.

Are the terms synonymous?

Another question I ask in my courses, is, 'Are the terms "stable" and "predictable" synonymous?' (I don't mean in a literary sense but in a business sense.) Most times the answer is 'no'. I then ask: 'Are the terms "unstable" and "unpredictable" synonymous?' Usually the answer is 'yes'. The idea is that unstable demand is probably unpredictable. I then ask the first question again: 'If "unstable" and "unpredictable" are synonymous, what about "stable" and "predictable"?' After some thought, I now get a lot more 'yeses'. So the objective is to get stable demand. By definition it will be more predictable. Attack things that cause unstable demand. It will be unpredictable.

Let's look at measurements

If the goal is stable, predictable demand, we ought to have a measurement system in place that rewards moving towards the goal and penalizes actions that move you away from the goal. However, it is a rare company that even measures the demand volatility in any meaningful way. What we *will* find are measurements that deliberately cause behavior that results in unstable, unpredictable demand.

A multitude of instability causes

Figure 2.8 shows some of the sales rocks in the lake. Several of these cause demand instability, simultaneously guaranteeing high inventories, poor customer service and excess costs. As mentioned earlier, I will cover some of these plus other causes of instability. I hope these trigger ideas for you to evaluate about *your* causes of instability.

Periodic sales targets

Most companies give their sales people targets for a period, such as a month or quarter. As long as the total sales are booked during this period, the sales person is a winner. It makes no difference when in the period the sales are made.

This process can give rise to some extremes in behavior, the most common one being what is called the hockey stick or banana curve of sales. Little or no sales occur early in the period, sales pick up a little in the middle to latter part of the period and then really go to town in the last few days. It is not unusual to see as much as 50% of the period's sales target booked in this last time slot.

A periodic sales target example

A large computer manufacturer in the North-East of America has a goal of shipping a complete mainframe computer 48 hours after receipt of order. This 48 hours is for final configuration to the customer's wishes plus test time. The computer has already been built up to a semi-finished state before the customer's order arrives. If we ignore the 48 hours for final configuration and test time, then order booking and shipping are synonymous.

The quarterly pattern of activities in this company is shown in Fig. 8.1. The numbers 1, 2, 3 are months during the quarter. As you can see, they regularly book 20% of the quarter's sales target in the first month of the quarter, 30% in the second and 50% in the third. These figures repeat regularly every quarter.

You can now see that the sales of mainframe computers are seasonal! It must be something to do with the wind, barometric pressure, sunspots or whatever, but of course it is not. It is simply that sales people are measured and rewarded by performance over the full quarter, hence they create volatility that causes sales in the last month of a quarter to be two and a half times the sales in the first month. How's that for induced volatility?

The factory's reaction is to even out production. You can make a company flexible, but not by two and a half times as much total production in one month as the next. So it produces about one-third of the budgeted production in the first month. This flows nicely into semi-finished inventory since all finished products are customer configured. Inventory levels at the end of the first month are equal to 13% of the quarter's production.

If you stand up on a bench about this time in the quarter and look out over the plant floor, as far as the eye can see there are almost finished computers. Consider the financial impact of all this inventory plus the additional square footage of building space that had to be built to accommodate the inventory. To earn an adequate return on assets, prices of the end products must be raised to pay for this unnecessary investment.

Production makes another third of the quarter's production in the second month, closely matching the sales that month. Then month three shows up.

	One quarter		
Months	1	2	3
Order booking	20%	30%	50%
Production	33%	33%	33%
Inventory	13%	16%	0

Fig. 8.1 Quarterly sales target.

In theory, it should make one third of the quarter's production and take the balance out of inventory to match the sales peak. The problem is, the computers in inventory were produced two months earlier to a sales forecast. Significant numbers of these computers are the wrong ones. Excessive overtime is needed to configure the semi-finished products to the customers' requirements plus reconfigure the wrong computers into the right ones. Quality suffers in this chaotic period, as evidenced by the warranty claims on products shipped in the third month of every quarter. Even with all this overtime, the company cannot meet its stated goal of shipment within 48 hours of receipt of order. Deliveries are late on a large percentage of products shipped in the third month.

What is stable demand?

Earlier, I said the objective was stable demand. I don't know what went through your mind then but you probably just accepted the term. It is now time to define it. Some people tell me it's the same demand every month, or the same every week, and they are on the right track. But the real answer is 'the same volume of demand placed on the business every day'. Most of the flexibility-enhancing techniques described earlier can accommodate a wildly fluctuating *mix* of products. Where they fall short is when the *volume* fluctuates.

Many people, especially those in sales, object to the time period of a day because of the variables in the market-place that they feel are uncontrollable. Of course, there is some basis for their objection. But how often do you measure the output from plant operations? For most companies, it is daily or even every shift. Some companies measure output every hour!

There are just as many variables affecting production as there are sales. Absenteeism, machine breakdowns, late vendor deliveries, emergency customer requirements, unexpected scrap and so on are all part and parcel of life in manufacturing. Measuring output daily and pushing for the same production every day has helped many companies reduce the incidence of these problems.

Measuring *sales* daily will have the same effect. Causes of peaks and valleys will be identified and solutions found. And the goal of the same volume of sales every day will be clear to everyone.

Promotions

Many companies periodically promote their products. They do this through special discounts for a period, coupons entitling the bearer to a lower price;

two for one sales and so on. Is this technique designed to give you stable, predictable demand? – no way. It is guaranteed to cause erratic, unpredictable demand. It pushes you away from your goal. Did the promotions you ran last year add to your financial results or detract? (This is another of the questions I ask in my seminars.) The answer? – 'I have no idea. We cannot measure that'.

What do you think about a business that employs marketing people to dream up promotions that cost the company money but they don't know if these efforts were financial winners or losers? On top of this they also made the market-place dynamic.

The roofing tile absurdity

A roofing tile company headquartered in the North Eastern part of America has many plants scattered across the United States. This is a seasonal business, especially in the northern states, not so much in the southern states. The peak season is late Spring, Summer and early Fall. Rain, snow and cold weather in the rest of the year dampen construction and repair work. During the slow period, the plants produce for inventory, but asphalt tiles are very heavy. You cannot stack them very high as the bottom tiles become deformed under the weight. So, in the slow period, they build as much as they can afford or the land they own can store.

During the peak season, they run the factories around the clock and sell out of the built-up inventory. But about midsummer all the inventory has been sold and now they go on back order. The factories cannot keep up with the peak demand.

When would *you* think would be a good time for a promotion? This company does it right in the middle of the summer when they already have more demand than they can handle! So they now sell this demand at a discount!

Back orders soar as incoming orders now far exceed plant capacity. Customer complaints increase because, inevitably, orders ship late. How's this for *profitably* delighting your customers? They are reducing profitability at the same time they are making customers upset, and making the seasonality peaks and valleys even worse.

A better idea would be to promote during the slow season. Customers would now inventory some of their product, allowing the total inventory build-up to be higher, smoothing out the summer peak. But promoting in the summer is what they have always done – customers expect it; competitors also do it. Who will have the courage to break this ridiculous process and move the business closer to its goal of stable, predictable demand?

Profitable promotions are few

Earlier I told you the answers I get to my question of whether the promotions you ran last year were profitable. 'I don't know' or 'We cannot measure that' are normal. Magid Abraham and Leonard Lodish, in their article, 'Getting the Most Out of Advertising and Promotion', *Harvard Business Review*, May–June 1990, refute this view. They created a scientific study to determine the financial results of promotions. Their findings? – 16% of trade promotions are profitable. For many promotions, the cost of an extra $1 of sales is *greater* than $1. This is by looking at the trading costs only. No factory costs are considered, such as working overtime to produce the extra product, maybe having a lay-off afterwards because of slow sales, the cost of the inventory build-up and so on. The 16% figure will obviously drop when all these production costs are factored in.

What if the promotion is more successful than you predicted? – you will probably go out-of-stock of this product. Scrambling the factory's schedules to rebuild the stock will cost *you* money.

What if the promotion is a dud? What do you do now with the extra inventory, fire sale it at a loss? It will cost you again. None of these issues is considered in the article's analysis but they are real concerns during all promotions. Some people might say, after reviewing this data, that promotional programs are employment programs for marketing people. Certainly, most promotions don't pay their way and, on top of this, they move you away from the goal of stable, predictable demand.

Why are promotions so bad? – because they motivate customers to buy ahead of their needs to gain the advantage of the promotion. Rarely do promotions increase total sales. They simply change the timing of when the sale will happen. This is especially true for established brands. You won't clean your teeth twice as often simply because you bought twice as much toothpaste during a two for one sale. You'll wait twice as long before replenishing.

Everyday low prices

Wal-Mart, mentioned earlier, has grown in 30 years to be the largest discount chain in the world. Its motto is 'Everyday low prices'. It avoids price promotions. Its financial results, relative to the world's previous largest discount chain, show twice the return on capital employed (ROCE).

One of the factors contributing to this financial superiority is its everyday low price strategy. Its inventory is significantly lower because its demand is stable and predictable. Its in-stock position is also better, for the same reason. So it gains incremental sales on a lower asset base, the best way of earning a higher ROCE.

Procter & Gamble is also moving away from promotions. A *Business Week* article, 17 February 1992, entitled 'Not Everyone Loves a Supermarket Special', states that 'wildly fluctuating prices boost the company's costs'.

Are all promotions bad?

Am I against all promotions? – of course not. The following promotions can make sense:

1   To help introduce a new product.
2   To clear out end-of-season inventory.
3   To clear out excess or slow moving inventory, especially just before the product is made obsolete.
4   To help even out sales of a seasonal product.
5   If they add tangible, bottom line results after all costs are considered.
6   As a defense against competitors' promotional activities.

This latter activity creates what is known as 'the war of the promotions'. You promote today and steal a little market share. Your competitor promotes tomorrow and steals it back. Total sales don't change, so all that occurs is less profitability for both parties. In some cases, Proctor & Gamble's prices have been lower with its everyday low pricing strategy than competitors' promotional prices! This has truly gained it market share.

Purchasing discounts

Many products have a sliding scale of prices depending on the quantity ordered. This is what is known as purchased price discounts. Does this strategy of selling give you stable, predictable demand? – no way. It deliberately causes peaks and valleys of demand.

If your customer wants 10 per week of a product, you have stable, predictable demand. It simply is not good business practice to say to him: 'Don't order in that way. Surprise me with an occasional order for 100 at a time and I'll give you a discount.'

The paper product story

One of my clients makes a paper product. It is sold to printers and converters who make labels for office products, consumer goods, medical supplies, etc. It used to sell product based on a published discount schedule:

the more you buy, the cheaper price per unit. The lowest price was obtained if you bought a truckload of paper. It only had a few customers large enough to buy in truckload quantities. Now and then, completely unpredicted, an order for a truckload would arrive. There was great rejoicing in the sales department because now it would meet its month's sales budget.

However, a truckload of one particular type of paper usually exceeded the normal quantity held in stock, so the warehouse sent all it had to this customer and put the balance on back order. Any other customers now wanting this product, even though they would pay a higher price, would also be put on back order or the sale would be lost. Being on back order was very negative to the plant so, with incremental costs, they broke into their schedules to produce more of this product to ship at the lowest possible price. Science at work!

Win/win becomes lose/lose

At face value, purchased discounts are win/win for both parties. The customer gets a lower price and the supplier makes a volume sale, allowing him to amortize his change-over costs over more units, lowering the total costs. In reality, it is lose/lose for both parties. What will the customer do with a truck load of paper? – unload it into his inventory, of course. He probably has no immediate need for the full truckload but the discounted price motivates him to buy this amount. So his inventory kicks up. He needs storage space for the inventory and must pay people for the material handling into the warehouse and then out again when he really needs the products. For the supplier, the unpredictable large orders *increase* total costs because of the disruption they cause and because they make other customers unhappy with their out-of-stock position.

This company has banned using purchased discounts as a way of incentivizing sales. It feels the negatives far outweigh the positives.

Incentivize to get stable, predictable demand

How could purchased discounts be used to give you demand that matched your goal? One way would be to give discounts based on the total purchased in a period, such as a year. You still might get an end-of-year spike in demand to meet some volume threshold where the discount is more favorable. But at least you would only get one peak and it would be fairly predictable.

You could have different year ends for major customers or sales territories. This way, all the end of year peaks wouldn't happen at once. Again, they would be fairly predictable and might be easily handled if the peaks occur at different times throughout the year. Rebates given, based on total sales in a period, such as a year, have a similar effect. Now that the order size has been eliminated as the decision point for the discount, customers can order more in line with their needs, which are bound to be more stable and predictable than when prompted by a discount offer. Customers still benefit from lower prices and avoid the warehousing, inventory and material handling costs; suppliers get annual volumes and stable, predictable demand. This has to be a win/win situation for all concerned.

Payment cycles

Many companies send out bills to their customers on dates unrelated to the shipment date. For example, some trade practices are that all deliveries up to and including the 25th of the month are billed at one time, on the 26th of the month. Payment terms are from the date of invoice, not the date of shipment. This has profound impacts on the ordering pattern of customers. If customers receive material on the 26th of the month, they get an additional 30 days free ride on the supplier's money, over and above the payment terms. If they receive material on the 25th of the month, they lose this 30-day benefit.

In this environment, orders peak up the day after the cut-off date and fall off significantly as the cut-off date approaches. This ordering pattern has nothing to do with real demand. It is induced by the financial benefit of the payment cycle.

A billing cycle example

A $1 billion North American division of a huge European corporation produces consumer electronics. These are sold out of its warehouses to distributors and retailers across the country. Its billing cycle is to issue invoices twice per month, around the 10th of the month and around the 25th – the exact dates depend on when weekends occur.

Their actual demand picture is shown in Fig. 8.2. The demand peak, equal to double the average demand, occurs on the 11th and 26th of each month. The low demand occurs on the 10th and 25th of each month, equal to one half the average demand. Swings in demand of 4 to 1 in a 15-day period are routine.

The company's stated goal is to ship products within 24 hours of receipt of order. It cannot do this during the peak periods, even with extensive overtime, thus upsetting customers with late deliveries. During the low

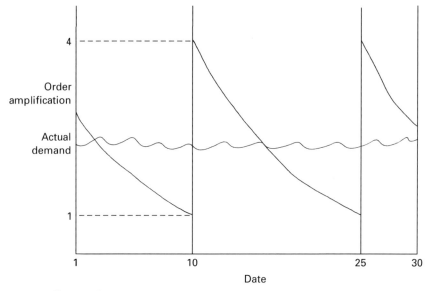

Fig. 8.2 Payment terms.

periods, the warehouse people try to look busy to avoid being sent home without pay.

The true demand for products is around the wavy line in the middle of the picture. Production rates are about the same but, because the actual ordering is distorted by the payment cycle, all products have to be sent to the warehouse, put away and then picked again to suit each sales order. If the ordering pattern was closer to the actual demand, many products, especially for large, regular customers, could be put on to trucks right off the end of the assembly line, bypassing the warehouse completely, with significant cost reductions.

The inventory levels could also reduce. Because of the peaks and valleys of ordering, buffer inventories are maintained to handle variations in the size of the peaks. And customers would get products routinely within 24 hours of placing their orders.

The solution is clear. Invoice daily for what was shipped that day. The problem is, this practice of billing twice per month is normal in the trade. If this one company goes to a daily invoicing cycle, they could get a lot of flack from their customers who in reality will lose 15 days free ride on this company's money. Lengthening the payment terms could offset this negative. So far, however, nothing has happened to change this ordering pattern. Customers and the manufacturer are content to live with the problem.

Inventory management systems that aren't

Several systems have been developed in the past 30 years, all with inventory reduction as one of their touted benefits. These systems have a variety of names, such as material requirements planning (MRP), manufacturing resource planning (MRP II), enterprise resource planning (ERP) and distribution requirements planning (DRP).

In reality, these are not inventory reduction systems at all, they are item management systems. They perform calculations to determine the demand for an item, its replenishment order size and its level of safety stock, if any. Replenishment lead time is frequently used as one of the factors in the safety stock calculation. Inventory planners receive the output from these calculations and then apply their judgment to decide exactly when and how much of each item to order. Such decisions are often modified again by purchasing people based on their knowledge of the market-place or specific supplier conditions.

Do these systems have the goal of giving a smooth, predictable demand to the supplier? – no way. In fact, they are designed to do just the opposite, give erratic, unpredictable demand. Do these systems really reduce total inventory? For some segments of inventory, the answer is 'yes'. For others, the answer is a resounding 'no'. Frequently they cause huge inventories to be held by both customer and supplier to buffer against the problems of supplying products with induced erratic, unpredictable demand.

Three examples of inventory system's erratic demand

I have selected three case studies from my client base to show how inventory systems give erratic demand and the solutions to this problem. Beware, you might get some violent reactions if you suggest to your customers that what I will explain is the real problem. I still bear the scars from the reactions I have received.

The 3M story

A division of 3M produced a product that was sold to equipment manufacturers who in turn sold this equipment to industrial consumers. One of these equipment manufacturers was large enough to have a significant impact on 3M's plant operations. 3M identified the impact as highly erratic demand from the customer. The customer identified the impact as 3M's poor delivery performance. 3M attempted to compensate for the demand variability by building inventory on overtime and reducing it on idle time.

Meanwhile, the customer alternated between inventory levels that were too high and what they perceived as poor customer service from 3M.

The customer demand history is shown in Fig. 8.3. The left-hand axis is not quantified but it does start at zero and shows how erratic the customer demand appeared according to 3M's records. This demand pattern was not repetitive so was completely unpredictable.

The materials managers at 3M and at the customer's plant met to solve the problem. The first question from 3M was, what was causing the demand from industrial consumers, the equipment manufacturer's customers, to be so erratic? Analysis showed this demand to be stable. So how can stable demand for the equipment manufacturer become erratic demand at 3M? The cause was identified as the manipulations which occurred between the equipment manufacturer's demand and orders placed on 3M. For example, if the equipment manufacturer decided to reduce inventory by two weeks' worth, 3M's monthly demand drops in half. Similarly, if it decided to increase inventory by two weeks' worth, 3M's monthly demand increased by 50%. Add to this decisions about the quantity to order, such as three month's worth this time, one month's worth next time, and you can see how demand for 3M can fluctuate by a factor of 10 to 1.

Why did these changes happen? Many of them are simply a function of item ordering systems. Today, many items need replenishing so demand is high. Tomorrow, few items reach their reordering position so total demand is low. Management concern regarding inventories puts pressure on the ordering clerks to order less. When this pressure is released, they revert to

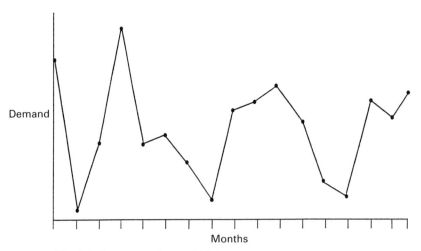

Fig. 8.3 Customer demand history.

their old ways and order more. Mathematics inside the reordering system change the timing when orders should be placed and the quantity to be ordered. These changes appear in total as greater or lesser demand, depending on the results of the calculations.

The solution was to remove the manipulations of their computerized inventory management system and all the extraneous input and pass demand cleanly from the equipment manufacturer to 3M. 3M's commitment was to deliver weekly quantities with a lead time of six days from receipt of order.

Figure 8.4 has the horizontal axis half the scale of Fig. 8.3. It repeats Fig. 8.3 first, then the demand after the new program started. The difference is startling. The result is that the equipment manufacturer's inventory turns on this material have increased from 8 to 50. 3M has shipped 100% on time since the program started. 3M has extended this program to all major customers, accounting for over 70% of their total demand.

A twist on twist drill bits

Cleveland Twist Drill (CTD) manufactures twist drill bits. They are sold through distributors to industrial customers and retail hardware stores. The company's problem was identical to 3M's. CTD had huge inventories but

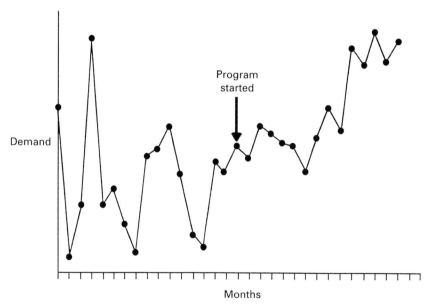

Fig. 8.4 Customer demand history – stabilized.

gave poor service to its customers. Its customers had huge inventories of CTD products but were often out-of-stock of specific sizes.

Analysis of CTD's demand pattern for a family of products, the most common family with the highest total sales, is shown in Fig. 8.5. This family consists of fractional, number and letter size drills. The variation in monthly demand is routinely 1.5 to 1 and can be as high as 2 to 1. Individual bit sizes within this family, even the most popular size which is quarter of an inch diameter, show month to month variations of 10 to 1. How can this be when the number of quarter-inch diameter holes drilled in America each day must be a reasonably stable number?

In this case the culprits are embedded mathematics in distributors' computer systems plus periodic reordering by retail stores and tool rooms. Many of the computer systems developed for distributors deliberately amplify small demand variations into huge supply variations. Couple this with unqualified people in charge of reordering and the problems can grow alarmingly.

The mathematics seem straightforward at face value. Assume demand for an item at a distributor increased this month by 5%. This means inventory dropped 5% more than expected, requiring a supply order to be generated sooner. The ordering quantity is a function of demand, so the amount ordered is increased. As twist drill bits are inexpensive, perhaps a normal order quantity is three month's worth of demand. So the lot size becomes 15% more this month. Safety stock is also a function of demand.

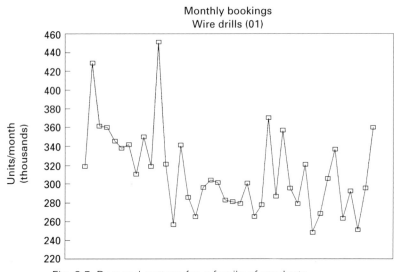

Fig. 8.5 Demand pattern for a family of products.

Say you plan to keep two weeks safety stock, but demand has gone up 5% so the quantity needed as a safety amount has increased by $2\frac{1}{2}$%. This behaves as if the inventory dropped a further $2\frac{1}{2}$% so must be replenished now. Add all these factors together, ordering sooner, ordering a larger lot and replenishing inventory and you can see how a 5% change in demand becomes a 20%-plus change in ordering. The reverse happens when demand drops 5%.

Now assume the distributor is replenishing from a regional warehouse. The warehouse has the same mathematical replenishment systems but the warehouse's demand has gone up 20% or more, the distributor replenishment order. The warehouse system processes the mathematics and orders 80% more from the central warehouse which uses the same mathematics. It in turn orders four times the normal monthly amount from the factory!

CTD decided, just as 3M did, to explain this phenomenon to its big distributors with the objective of coming up with a joint solution. I was chosen as the presenter of the phenomenon with CTD personnel demonstrating the actual volatility they were experiencing. The presentations were given at one of CTD's regular distributors' conferences and were slanted towards a win/win strategy. First, everyone carries less inventory. Second, everyone is able to give much better service to their customers.

The reaction from the distributors was disbelief. They could not accept that their systems of replenishment were the cause of the problem. We talked about working together for a common solution but the words fell on deaf ears. They refused to allow anyone from CTD near their operations to analyze whether the phenomenon was indeed happening or not or whether there was something else at fault. They blamed CTD for all their ills and said the solution was obviously for CTD to carry more inventory. We failed completely to get the message across. This program was stopped dead even though it would have given a win/win result.

In the soup with soup

Campbell Soup sells grocery items to retail chains. Customer service is critical in this business to ensure your product is pulled off the shelves by shoppers. Campbell Soup always had a high service level to its retailers' distribution centers but at a heavy cost of inventory and with frequent schedule revisions at the factory. All this was necessitated by the erratic ordering of the retail chains. Soup has a fairly stable end consumer demand so all the volatility of demand was added by the retail chain's ordering systems. In order to buffer themselves against the risk of stockouts, the retail chains also carried excess inventories.

To solve the problem and to lower total costs in the supply chain, Campbell Soup launched its continuous replenishment program with its largest retailers. This program started with Campbell establishing electronic data interchange (EDI) links with the retailers. Every morning, retailers electronically inform Campbell of their demand for their products and the level of inventories in their distribution centers. Campbell uses this information to decide which products need replenishing. Trucks leave the Campbell shipping plant that afternoon and arrive at the retailers' distribution centers, typically within 24 to 48 hours. As close as possible their motto is: 'Sell a case, replenish a case.' Don't allow embedded mathematics or people whims to distort the true demand.

Campbell's customer service has increased marginally but big gains have been made in inventory reduction, both at Campbell's warehouses and at its retail chain customers. This is a clear example of a win/win solution which profitably delights customers.

Miscellaneous other variability causes

Once you start digging you will find lots of other causes of induced demand variability. Here is a list of some of them:

1   Periodic advertising programs.
2   Sales people's commission plans.
3   Freight allowances.
4   Billing cycles.
5   Dating programs.
6   Product variety.

The key is first to measure your demand variability and then start digging for induced causes. Action programs to remove the offending policies or programs will result in a smoothing of demand with benefits to you and your customers.

Measuring demand variability

As just stated, the first thing you need to do is measure just how volatile your demand is. You'll be able to see then whether any fixes you put in have helped the situation.

Figure 8.6 shows the daily demand during a month for a product. As you can see it is quite erratic. Figure 8.7 shows this information put into a statistical distribution. The horizontal axis is a range of demand that was experienced, such as zero to 20 units, 20 to 40 units, and so on. The ver-

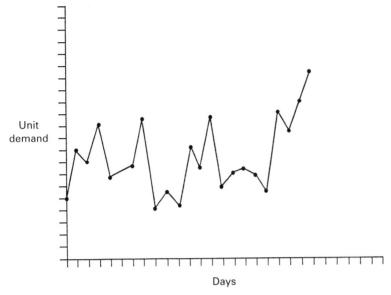

Fig. 8.6 Daily order pattern.

tical axis is the number of days in the month that demand fell within each range. For example, zero days had demand from zero to 20 units and 20 to 40 units, six days had demand between 40 to 60 units, etc. The chart clearly shows the variability in daily sales.

The objective is clear. As stated earlier, stable predictable demand is the same volume of sales every day. A bar 20 days high with the same range of units sold would be Utopia. Next month you would like to see again one bar a little to the right of this month's, the month after, the same again a little to the right again. This would show a stable, predictable, growing demand, a key objective to allow you to profitably delight your customers.

The way we were

A critical evaluation of the sequence in which companies should have responded to volatile demand suggests the following:

1 Address volatility causes, dampen where possible.
2 Increase plant flexibility to respond to demand variability.
3 Buffer volatile demand with inventory.

In reality, industry did exactly the reverse, aided and abetted by consultants and professional societies. I am one of the guilty parties. First, emphasis was placed on statistics to determine how much inventory would allow

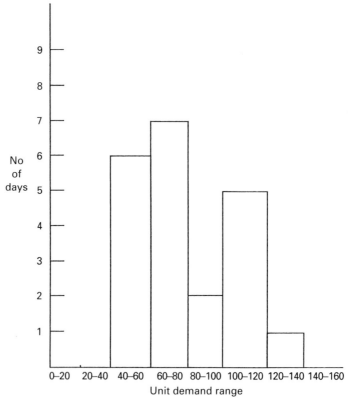

Fig. 8.7 Daily order distribution.

companies to give good customer service when faced with fluctuating demand. Second, making the factory flexible to respond to marketplace changes was the mantra. Just-in-time (JIT) concepts, MRP systems and their enhancements all relate to increasing flexibility to respond. Third, we are just now starting to address the causes of demand variability. It was always deemed to be uncontrollable, a function of the industry you were in. I hope the preceding thoughts about the causes of demand variability have persuaded you that much of demand volatility is induced and therefore can be dampened.

How should we use technology?

Earlier I talked about the problems of computerized inventory replenishment systems and gave examples of how they cause erratic, unpredictable demand. Embedded mathematics and human intervention can take stable demand from end consumers and create peaks and valleys for suppliers, the peaks and valleys becoming larger and larger as you move up the supply chain.

The solutions are inferred in the three examples. First, eliminate all the mathematics in the ordering process that manipulate when an item is ordered and how much is ordered. Second, remove human intervention from manipulating this data. Use computers, point of sale terminals and other technology to pass actual demand from the end consumer up the supply chain completely untouched. Have everyone follow the mantra: 'Sell one today, replenish one today.' In other words, replenish exactly what was sold, quickly. Everyone in the supply chain would now see the same demand as the end consumer, which is generally stable and predictable. All links in the supply chain would operate in lock step, delivering excellent service to the end consumer with rock bottom inventories and a stable, low cost, efficient operation.

9

Partnering for a win/win result

Partnering is the latest buzzword that describes relationships between companies. Unfortunately, the term has been used to cover a wide variety of practices, some detrimental as well as others that are positive. The detrimental school of thought uses 'partnering' as an umbrella term to cover another way of squeezing suppliers a little harder. They operate the relationship as a zero sum game. If one party gains advantage, the other loses.

The positive approach looks for ways in which, by working together, both or all parties gain incremental benefit. The concept is that, by blending the strengths of both parties, both become stronger so both gain advantages. The latter approach will be covered in this chapter.

The concept is not new. Many companies already have relationships with other companies that could be called partnerships, such as when sharing the costs of new research and development, in helping to market each other's products or to achieve global coverage. What is perhaps new about the concept is its application to the day-to-day operations of the business and its pervasiveness up and down the supply chain. More and more companies are realizing they cannot spread their limited resources, especially of scarce management talent, across non critical elements. They must focus the bulk of their effort on their core activities and give what is left to other companies which are better equipped to perform them.

Pushing the concept ahead is the realization that many manufacturing companies add only 20% of the value into a product. Fully 80% is purchased content. So for a variety of reasons, such as reduced costs, design help, flexibility, responsiveness and so on, it makes sense to elicit the help of those companies controlling 80% of the product value.

The ratio of value added internally versus purchased is the same regardless of where you are in the supply chain, so I am not just talking about end customers and the final manufacturing step here. The true partnering concept applies wherever you are positioned in the supply chain.

Taken to its extreme, which many groups of companies are working on, it applies to *all* links in the chain. Competition in the future will be supply chain versus supply chain. The goal will be to profitably delight the end consumer and, in so doing, profitably delight each link in the chain. Partnering will be a key activity to get this result.

Most writings focus on the customer in the customer vendor partnership. They describe his efforts and the benefits he will gain. But vendors have as much if not more to gain from true partnership relationships. They should be willing participants or even active proponents of this philosophy for the benefits *they* will gain of increased sales, reduced costs and lower assets and, even more importantly, of increased say over their future.

The partnering scenario

Figure 9.1 shows a variety of opportunities for partnering. Your company is in the middle labelled 'Us'n'. I couldn't think of a better term – 'We' sounded too innocuous. Most partnering activities occur with vendors, so are along the product flow axis. As every manufacturer is a customer and a supplier, then these areas are where most attention is directed.

'Them' means competitors. More and more partnering relationships are being formed between competing companies. The automobile industry is especially active in this, to fill out a product line, to invest in new facilities, share R&D expense, open a new market, etc. 'Services providers' can be either to help run the business, so the arrow points in, or to help market or distribute the product, so the arrow points out.

All these different options are available to a company to use and I am sure many readers recognize one or more of these that their company is currently using. The key is to use as many partnerships as makes sense, either to release management talent and resources to focus on your core

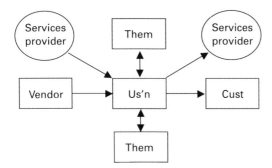

Fig. 9.1 The partnering scenario.

activities, for cost reduction or to get better business results than you could get alone.

Partnering defined

What sets partnering apart from standard procurement practices, either of materials, services or equipment? There are several answers. First, standard procurement is an arm's length process. An offer is made and either accepted or rejected. It is a simple buy/sell deal. Second, standard procurement is usually a short-term arrangement. This order or this annual quantity is covered. The next order or annual quantity can be renegotiated or the order given to some other company.

Third, with standard procurement, the vendor has little input to the product or service specifications. Fourth, with standard procurement, there is no ongoing dialog between buyer and seller on how they can help each other to both become more profitable.

Partnering reverses these statements. It is a close, long-term relationship where all parties work consistently together in creative ways so all become more profitable. Extensive two-way communication becomes the norm in this environment.

Underlying issues

The change from an adversarial relationship (standard procurement) to a partnership takes time. Historical behavior, where one party has taken advantage of another, will take time to wash out. Building up to a trust level where sensitive information can be shared openly won't happen overnight. However, trust, honesty and integrity are absolute necessities for partnering to work. They are also very frail commodities that can easily be destroyed by one false move.

This demands that decisions of whether to enter into partnering relationships or not, must be made at the very senior management levels of both parties. Without this backing, and a conduit for handling small glitches quickly, the relationship will soon break down. Senior managers must also buy into the fact that they are signing up to lose some of their autonomy. They can no longer make unilateral decisions that could affect the other party. Make sure this is understood and accepted by the senior people in both companies before proceeding. Failure to do this will doom the relationship as soon as a senior manager makes a decision harmful to the other party.

A damaging unilateral decision

One of my large conglomerate clients bought into the idea of partnering. It had active programs going within several of its divisions for three years. Considerable progress was made. The general manager retired and was replaced by an outsider. Shortly afterwards, the new GM went to Wall Street and spoke to some analysts. His question was: 'Why is my company's stock price low?' The answer: 'Inadequate return on assets.' I am sure it will come as no surprise to learn that a good part of the GM's annual bonus was based on stock price.

On his return to the corporate headquarters, he dashed off a memo to each of his divisions' presidents: 'Instead of paying suppliers in 30 days, now pay in 60 days.' The presidents objected to this pronouncement, telling the new GM about their supplier partnership program. Their pleas fell on deaf ears, so they had no choice but to change their payment practice. This action extended the liabilities so reduced the net assets of the business, hence the company's return on assets should have improved.

Imagine the reaction from their suppliers. Some were small companies that had a significant share of their business with this conglomerate. They couldn't afford to refuse this business, but now they were forced to extend their financing. Other, larger suppliers were not so beholden.

Their reaction was to lower the priority of this company's orders. Deliveries now were often late and the partnering activities were terminated. Still other large suppliers said they would no longer do business with this company. Three years of hard work by a large number of people in this company and with their suppliers was destroyed by one unilateral decision. And, because of the poor delivery performance of a few critical vendors, shipments to customers were often delayed because of shortages. The planned increase in return on assets in fact did not happen.

The second GM has now been replaced by another. He is interested in establishing partnerships with his divisions' suppliers. You can imagine the reaction from the staff in his divisions and in their suppliers. It will be a long, tough road to establish anywhere near the partnership relationships which existed previously.

Reducing costs

It must be made clear up front that one of the key objectives of the partnership is to reduce costs, especially NVAW costs. This will not create a country club atmosphere with everyone taking it easy now they are

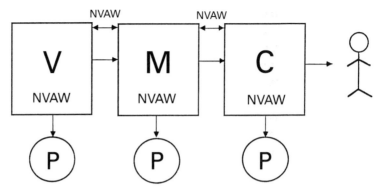

Fig. 9.2 A value or supply chain.

partners, just the opposite. The idea is to increase the intensity of cost reduction.

Figure 9.2 shows a simple value or supply chain. 'V' stands for a vendor delivering materials or parts to a manufacturer labelled 'M' who in turn serves 'C', another manufacturer, distributor or retailer, who sells to his customer, the stick figure. If each conducts business at an arm's length, all three companies' objectives are to maximize their profits, marked 'P'. This may be done at the expense of the others in the chain. Hence the total profit earned by the chain is the sum of the three 'P's.

If you look at the picture globally, however, it is obvious that the selling price to C's customer, the stick figure, is relatively fixed, by competition, the market-place and so on. All activities leading to this customer should be considered as costs. The three parties in the value/supply chain should work together to reduce the total chain costs so that the pie of profits earned by the chain *in total* is maximized. Without question, there now has to be an allocation of these profits back to the individual companies in the chain. But, if they are successful, the profit earned by each company in the chain will be more than the profit they would have earned when acting independently.

Theory versus reality

The above is the theory of partnering. Does it make sense? – undoubtedly. Does it work? – only in about 20% of the companies claiming to use partnering. Why, because of a faulty theory? – no way, it is because of people. Some people find it hard to resist taking advantage of the other party, especially when they are being pushed hard to meet narrow company performance objectives.

Others don't like the restraints that partnering imposes. Still others cannot behave ethically. They blab confidential information released to them by one of their partners to that partner's competitors. No doubt there are other reasons, but they all boil down to people and ethical behavior. Make sure these issues are clearly understood by everybody in your company and your potential partners' company before proceeding – set up a code of conduct for everyone in both companies to conform to. You will still get some problems but if the senior managers of both parties react quickly to snuff out any small fires, you will, in time, be able to form a fully fledged partnership relationship.

Is it for everyone?

In any activity, a few aspects tend to be important. The 80/20 or Pareto rule states that maximum gain will be made by focusing attention on the important things which are, in the case of the value/supply chain, vendors and customers that account for most purchases or most sales. Don't spread yourself too thinly by trying to involve all your customers and vendors in this type of relationship. Many of them cannot give you the business return for the needed effort.

Levels of partnering

As mentioned above, partnering is not something you want to work on with all suppliers. Most attention should be applied where maximum results can be gained, that is, on the most important suppliers. But some partnering actions could be beneficial with some less important vendors. This suggests different levels of partnering. For example, for a level one vendor, you would probably want to establish a full partnership. This could include having the vendor design specific parts for your products, having him build facilities close to your plants, having common investment and business strategies, promoting each other's products with other parties, sharing sensitive cost, profitability and investment information, having multiple cross business teams working to reduce costs, improve flexibility, increase responsiveness, etc.

For a level two vendor, you would probably want to establish a partial partnership. The effort to establish a full partnership with this vendor would not be worth the payback. Partnering in this case could consist of quality certified products delivered to point of use, limited technical help in design, a strong focus on cost reduction, kanban replenishment, etc. Level three vendors would normally be commodity manufacturers. Annual contracting with automatic replenishment or an in-plant store would suffice here.

Reducing NVAW

As mentioned earlier, one of the key objectives of partnering is to reduce costs, especially NVAW. It has been estimated by some companies that NVAW approximates 40% of total business costs for a manufacturer. If you accept this figure, for every $1 spent with vendors you are paying 40 cents for his NVAW! It has also been estimated that with a focused effort, NVAW can be reduced by half in 12 to 18 months.

The key words here are 'focused effort'. NVAW is entrenched in every aspect of the business – rooting it out will be quite a challenge. It is also true that some companies have already done a lot of work to reduce NVAW. They have used a variety of techniques, such as process mapping, to illustrate all business processes and, in the process, identify NVAW activities. Redesigning the process to clean out as much NVAW as is thought possible completes the job.

What if your vendors or customers have not progressed this far? Then, referring back to Fig. 9.2, the job of the advanced company is to cajole, teach and even provide technical help to reduce the laggard companies' NVAW so that total costs reduce, providing a bigger pie of profits for all to share.

NVAW is also given by the supply chain partners *to* each other. Many times, the specifications provided by the buyer to the seller are too tight or unnecessary. Costs are inflated because of this. That is why, as much as possible, vendors should design the parts customers need. The vendor knows most about the characteristics of his products so is in the best position to design cost-effectively. The customer simply provides the operating specifications and shape envelope to the vendor.

NVAW can also be created in the relationship with vendors, where purchase orders, packing slips, receiving reports, invoicing, incoming inspection, stores and so on are all NVAW. More streamlined buying, such as kanban replenishment or vendor restocking, as in a supermarket, can reduce ordering costs and time. Quality certified products delivered to point of use can reduce receiving inspection, stores and material handling costs. Electronic payment, paying vendors monthly or paying by company credit card, rather than producing a check for every delivery, can reduce the payment costs.

To eliminate many of these inter-company NVAW issues, though, is going to require cross-company teams and open minds in both companies, especially where these changes may be thought of as loss of control.

The case for partners as sole source suppliers

The idea of a sole source vendor sends chills down the backs of many manufacturing and purchasing people. Their immediate concern is interrupted supply, from fires, strikes, floods, etc. The assumption is that multiple vendors provide safety against supply interruption, which of course is true up to a point. Assume you have two vendors for an item, one supplying 60% of your needs, the other 40%. If the 60% vendor shuts down, for whatever reason, it is unlikely the 40% vendor will be able to quickly increase production to cover the lost 60%. Material supply, capacity and labor all take time to adjust. So did you really have protection or just the incremental cost of dealing with two vendors?

How do you get a full partnership with dual vendors? Each one knows you could put more or less business their way. How much investment will a vendor make in your business under these uncertain relationships? Will he assign his best talent to work on your new product design or someone of lesser importance? What would *you* do under these conditions? My guess is you would not be a fully committed partner. I doubt partnering would flourish under this scenario.

So what about the risk of a sole source vendor? How can it be minimized? Well, the first thing is to have a two-way dialog about this early on in the partnership discussion. What about your plant? Could you be shut down because of a strike, fire, flood, etc? Doesn't the vendor want protection against these events if he becomes a partner?

A sole source vendor doesn't necessarily mean a single plant. A vendor with multiple plants producing the same or similar items provides the same protection as multiple vendors without the attendant costs. How acrimonious or friendly are the employee/management relations? Is the risk of a work stoppage so remote as to be insignificant?

There is no black and white answer to the sole source/multiple vendor issue. Don't let emotion rule. Discuss the issue logically from both sides, estimate risks, look at the probability of successful partnering with either approach and make a reasoned decision.

Partners on your design team

I mentioned in Chapter 5, during the discussion of concurrent engineering, that customers and vendors should be part of your design teams. Customers who contribute to a product's design details become emotionally linked to the product, so are more likely to buy it. On top of this, they help make the product more successful as their requirements are also likely to be similar to those of other customers.

Earlier in this chapter I mentioned that manufacturers typically add only 20% of the value in a product, fully 80% is purchased. This statistic alone cries out for you to get more vendor help in design. With a partnership relationship, this help will be willingly given. After all, it is a win/win decision. But now the ethics are that this vendor, who helped design some parts for your products, also be asked to produce them. Contrast this to another company that I heard about recently who persuaded a vendor to help it design its products. They then took this vendor's designs for their parts and sent them out to multiple vendors for competitive bid! I am sure they will get a lot of talented help from this vendor on their next product design! You can see this company's emphasis is on taking advantage of their suppliers for a win/lose result. Even worse, some of the customer's senior managers felt there was nothing wrong with this way of behaving.

Chapter 5 examined the benefits of being 'quick-to-market' rather than being 'johnny come lately'. Vendors can be critical allies in rapid product development. Your time to market will shrink appreciably if you involve your vendors early on in such things as designing and building tooling, ordering raw materials, etc.

A design partnership case study

A *Managing Automation* article described how Solaris, a Monsanto Company division, designed a new sprayer system. Only two months into the development of the idea, Solaris had selected the vendors, known as 'the chosen ones'. Solaris was able to review the pros and cons of various design ideas directly with the vendors responsible for manufacture and assembly of the end product. Design information was transferred via computer aided design (CAD) files, eliminating the need for formal document processing and drawings. Trust between the company and vendors was so strong that much of the information necessary to manufacture the product was communicated informally. The net result: a quicker time to market.

Opening communication channels

Partnering demands a much higher level of dialog between the partners, both in volume and in the depth of information provided. This will take time to occur. Most partnerships start out with little more information flow than when they operated at arm's length. But, in time, it becomes obvious to both parties that, to be successful, a lot more information should be shared. Early on, this will be operating information, such as production schedules, quality criteria, cost reduction and so on. It will then progress into the design area, ways to enhance flexibility, and business strategy. Later still, cost information, planned investments, expansion plans, etc, will be shared.

The key word here is shared. This means the same information is available and presented by each to the other. Compare this to one company that recently demanded their vendors show them detailed cost information. They refused to reciprocate. That is *not* a partnership.

Many people will be uncomfortable with the idea of sharing what today they consider confidential information which could be leaked to competitors or used against them. Such concerns can only be overcome by spending the time to develop the necessary trust and by making a visible and dependable commitment to an ethical approach. As mentioned earlier, the first stages of enhanced communication will be about operating issues. As time goes by and trust grows, more sensitive information is shared. As long as nothing occurs to destroy the trust, then more and more sensitive information will change hands.

Earlier I talked about the idea that the role of partners in a supply chain is to increase the pie of profits available to the chain. At some time, then, these increased profits must be allocated back to the individual partners. It will be difficult to do this equitably without having all financial information about each of the partners on the table. What upcoming investment programs are necessary in each of the companies? How much R&D is required? What other expenses relative to the supply chain's success are needed? And what level of ROI does each need to satisfy shareholders? Only when such detailed financial information is freely shared can the profits of the chain be divided fairly among its members.

Trust requires management stability

Trust is something that exists between two people. It cannot be written into a legal document. It is an eyeball to eyeball feeling. Replace one of the two people and the trust relationship has to start over again. Changes in management, especially of the very senior people, have to be made with the impact on trust in mind. Partnerships develop because chief executive officers feel comfortable working together, as do the people at lower levels of management. Lessons learnt from successful German companies, as reported in a recent *Harvard Business Review* article, are that continuity of people make relationships work. This means that CEOs must spend more time managing inter-company relationships.

I am sure that, based on my earlier comments, you can see the need for multiple links between organizations. The links will be: systems experts planning data interchange capability; manufacturing people agreeing on scheduling processes and quality standards; designers working together to design products; finance people arranging billing procedures and so on. One CEO jokes that he used to have only one extra chair in his office. For any decision today his office is crowded, with 'outsiders' included.

Starting a seven-step partnering program

I'll assume your senior managers have recognized the benefits of partnering and that they are willing to abide by the restraints such a program creates, even if it means giving up some of their autonomy. If this is not the case, don't embark on a partnering program. You will waste a lot of time and only foster ill will.

Step one – develop a check-list

This is a list of some of the parameters within which a partnership has to work and includes the following agreed minimum performance levels:

1 Technical capability now and in the future.
2 Capacity to produce your needed volumes.
3 Investment in equipment to improve productivity and for future expansion.
4 Agreed quality performance as a total business concept.
5 Suitable financial strength.
6 Agreement to conduct an ethical relationship, particularly from senior management.
7 Coherent long-term business strategies.

I am sure you can think of other issues unique to your business that should also be on the check-list.

Step two – select the first few potential partners

These will probably come from your existing base of vendors or customers, people you have dealt with for a long time and have a good working relationship with. Choose those companies that you feel have the best people, because partnering is a people issue. You will have a much higher chance of success working with good people.

Step three – conduct an education/training program

This should be with your key people and with the key people from your potential partners. The idea here is to share your understanding of the pros and cons of partnering and to get buy-in from all levels of management.

Step four – audit the first potential partner

Don't be surprised if the potential partner also wants to audit you. That would show they have understood the two-way process of partnering. Be wary of just looking at today's performance. You should be most interested in the potential and drive for improvement in performance. Rate characteristics first on this basis, second on their current performance.

Step five – revise the audit checklist

You will learn during the first audit that elements of your checklist are inadequate or superfluous. Modify it before continuing to audit other potential partners.

Step six – expand as resources and knowledge allow

Be cautious about taking on more potential partners too soon. You have a lot to learn about working with partners. The process will also demand a lot of time from many different people in your organization, so make sure you don't take on too many prospects too soon.

Step seven – develop the partnerships over time

As mentioned several times, partnering is a growing experience. Keep reviewing progress, willingness on both sides to improve and the growth of trust. Add other areas of co-operation when the conditions are right.

Working this process enables everyone in the partnership to profitably delight their customers and most of all, the end customer in the value chain, the truly important customer to all parties.

Reducing the vendor and customer base

I am sure that, as you read this chapter, you realized that partnering cannot be employed with a large number of vendors or customers. The intensity of communications and demands on people resources preclude this. Following this realization, most companies start, in parallel with partnering, a vendor reduction program. As an example, Rover cars a few years ago had 2000 suppliers. The figure today is less than 500 with an immediate target of 300. Rover and its suppliers are working in what they call the extended enterprise. The benefits have reportedly been dramatic in terms of reducing costs. A number of other companies have results similar to this.

Few companies have started a customer reduction program, holding to the idea they have never seen a customer's order they didn't like. But it is obvious that partnering will demand you work with a limited number of customers, for the same reasons mentioned earlier. One company that has realized this is Nypro, a plastic parts molder with 14 plants worldwide. Ten years ago it had 600 customers and gross sales of $66 million. Today it grosses three times as much. Thirty major companies account for 80% of sales. Nypro selected customers from industries which valued Nypro's ability to produce to tight tolerances with outstanding quality that was medically clean. It doesn't target industries that are simply buying on price. Its sales growth, profit growth and return on assets are three times the industry standard.

10

Ever more changes

Old ways of doing business will not suffice for the future. The industrial scene has changed and will continue to change as the less developed countries elbow their way into traditional markets. In such a scenario, change will be the only constant on which you can rely. New ways must be found in order to survive and prosper in the future, and my view is that customer focus will be one, if not the most important, route to achieving sustained prosperity.

Let me describe some of the issues, presently in their early stages or on the horizon, which will affect every manufacturer. Make sure you are working on these, as well as those described in earlier chapters, to exploit to the full their potential for achieving the best possible customer satisfaction while, at the same time, minimizing your own costs.

Surprises in global manufacture

Over the last few years, companies have been looking beyond their own shores in the search for cheaper labor costs and new markets – radical change has occurred in the geographical location of manufacturing facilities. So first, let's examine a few of the terms which have very quickly infiltrated into manufacturing terminology and which exemplify the way that change is happening:

'Onshore' means producing close to or in the market-place you're trying to serve. 'Offshore' means producing a considerable distance away from the target market-place, probably across a sea. You plan to export into that market-place. Producing in Europe for Europeans or in America for Americans are both onshore by these definitions. Producing in Singapore for Europeans or in Mexico for Japanese is offshore. I will modify both these definitions a little later.

The ping pong of plant location

Prior to 1950, most plants were situated in the markets they served. I call this local for local. Because of huge tariff barriers at country borders, it was almost impossible to compete by producing in one country for sale in another, because the tariff mark-up made most imported products too expensive. Then along came the European Common Market in 1952. The first 12 countries joined together to create a union that would rival the American States. Tariff reduction between the member countries, one of the earlier agenda issues, was quickly implemented. In 1962, the Kennedy round of the General Agreement on Tariffs and Trade (GATT) initiated significant reductions in tariffs around the world. Subsequent meetings of this group have slowly whittled away tariffs on almost all manufactured goods.

These two events led most major companies to search for low cost manufacturing locations anywhere in the world. The stampede to go offshore or remote from the target marketplace started in earnest. Plants sprang up in several of the less developed countries, such as Taiwan, Singapore and Korea, and offshore sourcing was done in such places as India and China. The left-hand side of Fig. 10.1 shows this movement from local for local to low wage rate countries.

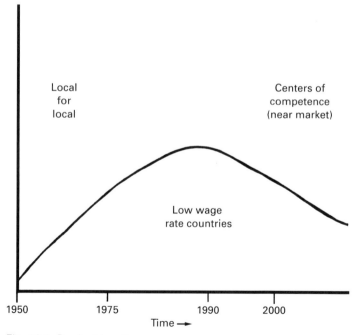

Fig. 10.1 Product location.

This wave of change has now run its course. I predict the export and import of manufactured goods, especially across seas, is now at its peak. A move is just starting to go back to producing and sourcing in or close to the marketplace, in what is termed in Fig. 10.1 as 'centers of competence'. This will not mean a return to local for local but a significant reduction in manufactured goods travelling by sea. There are multiple reasons to produce onshore:

Reason one: distribution versus wage costs

Distribution costs per product are slowly climbing. Customs brokers, stevedores, transportation companies, customs agents, etc, all get involved in moving goods by sea. These are outside a company's direct control so this rise in costs cannot be subject to the same kind of cost containment activities that can occur within the company.

Wage costs per product in the producing country, on the other hand, are static or in some cases, most notably electronics, even reducing. Productivity, new designs and new processes all work to limit the wage costs per product. This relationship between distribution and wage costs is shown diagrammatically in Fig. 10.2. The slope of the distribution costs lines is not drawn to scale but exaggerated to show the concept.

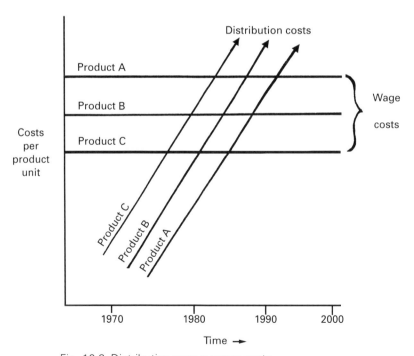

Fig. 10.2 Distribution versus wage costs.

As you can see, the distribution cost line for a product crosses over its wage cost line at some point. As soon as this increase in distribution costs exceeds the savings in offshore wage costs, production would be most economical closer to the market or onshore.

Eventually, all products will reach this point except aircraft and ships. The timing will be controlled by the value density of the product. Bulky, low cost products, such as washing machines, refrigerators, clothes dryers, etc, are rarely produced offshore because of the distribution/wage cost relationship. Automobile final assembly, where most of the bulk occurs, is also being carried out more and more often onshore for the same reason. Automobile components, such as engines, transmissions, etc, are still being made offshore because the value density is high. In time, even these components will be made onshore as the distribution/wage cost relationship changes.

Automation of manufacturing is accelerating this trend. Automation reduces wage costs so the choice of manufacturing location has little or nothing to do with wages. Accessibility to cheap financing and technically trained people are the determinants of location. These will generally be found in the world's major markets of Europe, America and Japan.

Nicholas Hayek, Swatch's general manager, states that when wage costs per product drop below 10% of sales value, production can be done anywhere in the world cost effectively. He prefers to make watches in Switzerland, a high wage rate country, because of its people's technical competency and easy access to financing.

Reason two: speed of response

Customers want what they want immediately. We might sneer at this instant gratification trend but we are all part of it. Customers want lead times for almost all products to be shorter, even those that are custom made. This is forcing a drastic re-evaluation by many companies of where to site various elements of production. For example, one of my clients, with plants in Australia, Europe and America, makes large rolls of a paper sandwich which are then slit and wound into various widths and lengths. Customers buy these slit rolls for further processing.

Some widths and lengths are what this company calls standard. They stock these in several locations strategically located to serve local markets. Other widths and lengths are non-standard so are made to order. The company is seeing a significant increase in the demand for non-standard slit rolls because their customers want to reduce the amount of waste they create when using standard rolls. But, to get a non-standard roll slit at the factory and then shipped to the customer, takes much longer than the customer expects to wait.

To react, this company is moving all slitting operations into the warehouses. It now only makes the large rolls of the paper sandwich at its factories. Now it has done this, there is almost no need for standard slit rolls to be held in inventory. Its total inventories have dropped as it has increased speed of response to customers' needs.

In this case, the terms offshore and onshore mean something slightly different. Offshore simply means remote and onshore means close to the marketplace. Remote is defined as too far away to respond to customer needs, regardless of whether that is across seas or on land. The message is, site your manufacturing sources where they will achieve maximum customer satisfaction. This company is now beginning to question whether the large rolls of the paper sandwich should be produced in one central factory or produced in smaller factories close to the marketplace, as well as whether its drive in the past for wider, faster, larger roll makers was correct. For some products it would probably be beneficial to have small, flexible roll makers in the warehouses to be able to vary quickly the components of the paper sandwich to suit different customer needs.

Reason three: shorter life cycles

Almost all products are being made obsolete and replaced at an ever increasing speed. Even those that are not obsolete are receiving frequent upgrades to keep interest high in the marketplace and to take advantage of the latest technology.

Producing offshore creates two problems in this environment. First, communicating and implementing the changed design usually takes longer. Second, the pipeline of products in transit and in inventory must clear before the new or revised product can be offered. More nimble competitors can have their new designs in the marketplace first, gaining a significant competitive edge.

Miscellaneous issues

Many other concerns are pushing the movement of production closer to the target sales area. I will quickly touch on a few that may or may not apply to every case. Overheads will grow to manage an offshore facility. Communications, additional paperwork, visitations by people from both sites, and increased inventories will all demand resources. The problem is that most of this additional work will be hard to quantify as it will be small pieces of time spread over many people. But, make no mistake, overhead costs will grow.

Different languages and cultures will give rise to misunderstandings and errors. Time zones often will make it difficult to converse with a particular person.

Social issues can sometimes backfire. The recently publicized issue of children working in offshore factories to produce low cost clothing and shoes has hurt the affected companies.

Inflation and exchange rates can quickly erode the projected savings from any offshore facility. Moving the assets to the next low cost area won't be easy or cheap.

Some telling comments

Dick Morely of Modicon says: 'Some manufacturing was sent offshore to capture lower labor costs, with offsetting problems in materials, WIP, and bulging inventory pipelines. Add to this the challenge of quickly and effectively executing an engineering change order, and we knew something had to give.' The company woke up and brought manufacturing and service back to the United States.

Mike Wicken of Toyoda Machinery USA states: 'I need to be able to respond quickly to the demands of the customer. You can't do that by shipping in fully built-up units. You can only be that responsive by manufacturing *right here.*'

Does offshore manufacturing have a future?

The pressures mentioned earlier will continue to erode the value of producing or sourcing somewhere remote from the market-place. But there are still times when offshore manufacturing is the correct choice. Sometimes the cost differential is so great it is a no-brainer to produce or source offshore. One of my clients calculates the indirect costs of sourcing offshore are 22% to 30%. He sets a guideline that he needs to save this percentage plus another 10% to profit from offshore sourcing, and there are times that he is able to do this.

Reciprocity, where there is a law or local government pressure forcing you to build in a country to be able to sell in that same country sometimes causes plants to be sited in uneconomical locations. It's not a choice if you want to participate in that market-place.

As a stepping stone to being an onshore facility you might go offshore for a while. This seeming contradiction means to build a plant in an area that is not yet a market-place but has the potential to be one. So you build there and export most of the production. As the local market develops, you sell more production locally. By being there early on, before it's a good market-place, you build a reputation that helps when you sell locally.

Perhaps the technology you need is only available in a certain country. You are forced to source from this offshore location. There may be other exceptional conditions that require you to produce or source offshore. These will become fewer and fewer for the reasons mentioned earlier. In time, almost all products will be produced close to or in their market-place.

A looming social problem

Many of the less developed countries are counting on manufacturing to employ their large numbers of unemployed people. They also expect to earn hard currency by exporting to the wealthier nations, but this is not going to happen. Manufacturing will employ fewer and fewer people with plants located close to the major market-places. Unless the LDCs can become market-places they will become poorer while the wealthy nations become richer, and the chance of them becoming market-places is slim. To become a market-place you need population and cash. The LDCs have the first, not the second. So a potential Catch 22 is developing for the LDCs. Make sure you are aware of its attendant implications.

Professor Hasegawa of Waseda University is concerned about ' . . . the impact of vast productive capacity with little work force. Most importantly, is the reversal of movement of industrial work back to the already developed nations because of capital and skilled work force, thus making the earnings difference between these and the less developed nations even greater'. He draws a corollary between agriculture and manufacturing. At one time, agriculture was the dominant employer. Today it employs a few percent of the population and often even this few is too much, reference the 'set aside' programs in America and the mountains of excess foodstuffs in Europe. Today, manufacturing is a significant employer but its percentage and absolute numbers are decreasing. This trend will continue forever and doesn't leave much hope for the LDCs without huge gifts of cash from the wealthy countries to the poor ones.

The virtual corporation

Many companies are outsourcing many of their activities, reducing their internal actions down to what they consider is their core competency. Other reasons for working with other companies were given in Chapter 9.

Technology, especially of communications, is enabling companies in distant locations to work together almost as if they were right next door. This is the essence of virtual corporations, a network of companies situated anywhere in the world, linked together with communications and other technology so they operate as one unit.

This is not necessarily an extension of partnering, as described in Chapter 9. For one thing, many virtual corporations will be formed to address a specific issue, such as a market-place opportunity, a technology development program, etc, and, when complete, disbanded. Second, many of these networks will move information, not products. As described earlier, moving products large distances is becoming passé, but information can move anywhere in the world almost for free and this can be exploited to maximize customer satisfaction. A global design team, in touch and working 24 hours a day, might win you lots of customers by coming up with quick solutions to a need for changes to a component's design. A global network of on-line suppliers whose inventory you can instantly access might win you a contract for quick completion of an order. An off-shore marketing facility might enable you to exploit a fashion fad or fill a gap in the world market for a specific material of which you happen to have large stocks.

Fluidity will be the key because virtual corporations that are short-lived will operate much more on a contractual, not a trust, basis. The lead corporation will search out the best companies to participate in a given project and contract with them for a set of deliverables. Frequent communications among the network of companies will keep all facets of the program coherent.

You should be aware of the largest problem slowing down this scenario – the incompatibility of technology. We all expect telephones anywhere in the world to link together. Unfortunately, this is not the way computers and many aspects of software behave. And, as with telephones, the fact they link together still doesn't mean communications happen. If you are only fluent in English and the other party you have called is only fluent in German, then information transfer doesn't happen. All you get is a babble of noise. The same is true with information sharing with computers. Incompatibility of CAD systems, data files, nomenclature and so on make sharing information among companies slow and error prone. This will change as more standards for interconnectivity are developed and implemented.

Another concern is security of information as it is sent electronically. This is a technical issue that will be solved soon to remove this constraint.

The agile corporation

Many aspects of the agile corporation are the same as a virtual corporation. Many books have been written on what agility means but, taken to its extreme, agility means the ability to design and make anything a customer wants, immediately. An illustrative example of agility is the three-day car – a car custom built and delivered three days after it is ordered.

Agility strikes at many aspects of current manufacturing technology. It includes reducing design cycle times, sharing information with suppliers, using modular components, and simplifying tooling to facilitate reusable designs, universal components and fixtureless machining. Rapid prototyping will be extended so that actual parts can be built up, layer by layer, which will actually function with minimal additional machining. This is in its infancy today.

Agility means that mass production in huge factories will be a way of the past. I predict that small factories located in or near the target market-place, as mentioned earlier, will become the norm. These factories will be surrounded by their suppliers and other support groups, such as tool and die builders, machine tool builders, etc. These companies will all be networked together and function as the virtual corporation mentioned earlier.

A virtual agile corporation

The Agile Web in Pennsylvania is an example of a virtual agile corporation. Nineteen manufacturing companies, consisting of machine shops, sheet metal shops, paint shops and printed circuit board manufacturers are linked in a consortium that can bid on jobs that none of the individual companies could tackle on their own. These firms are still competitors for normal business. Their major achievement, therefore, has been to work out the business relationships and processes that enable them to function co-operatively as well as competitively. Consider the amount of sensitive information that had to be shared the first time they priced as a team! They have since created a process for rapid partnering agreements, finance and accounting procedures and the handling of the intellectual property.

Needed: A few good people

The numbers of people employed in manufacturing in the industrialized countries has been declining in both percentage and absolute numbers since 1979. This has happened at the same time as manufacturing output has stayed steady as a percent of gross domestic product (GDP). Productivity has been the reason for this change. As an example, manufacturing productivity gains in America have averaged over three percent the last 15 years while GDP growth has been about two percent. The manufacturing workforce has declined one percent a year for the last 15 years.

This trend will continue, perhaps even accelerate. This is part of the reason for the earlier section, 'A looming social problem'. What about those people who are left in manufacturing? Their smaller number will give them much greater influence on customer satisfaction, meaning they will need quite different skills, knowledge and abilities than they do today. First, they will need a broader understanding of the business in total. The days when you could build a career by being expert in one business function, such as sales, design or accounting will be long gone. To be fast and responsive to customers' needs will require an elimination of many of the hand-offs that occur today between people in different business functions. Some of this 'knowledge' will be system generated.

Conceptualize a design engineer working on a variation of a product for a specific customer. The correct system support will perform a credit check on this customer and then estimate the costs of various design scenarios, allowing the engineer to pick the lowest cost choice. The system will then create the manufacturing instructions, purchase the needed materials and components, calculate the delivery date and relay the selling price and delivery to the customer. This could all be done without any hand-off to others.

Secondly, people employed in manufacturing companies will be team players in the fullest sense of the word. They will need to co-ordinate and be part of the virtual corporation system. This means working across company ownership boundaries as easily as working across internal departmental boundaries.

Thirdly, they will be much better technologists. Technology will be the backbone of the agile, virtual corporation. Two classes of technologists will be needed, those who can develop and implement new technology and those who will be able to use it to the fullest extent.

Fourthly, they will respect diversity, of opinions, culture and behavior. People from all backgrounds, nations and races will be part of the virtual corporation. Getting the most out of these people will mean being aware of fundamental differences in beliefs and patterns of thought, and then melding these together into a successful business.

Fifthly, they will be globally aware. They will need routinely to answer such questions, as 'Where is the best talent to provide this piece of technology?' 'Where should we site the new production facility to address this target market?' 'Where should we source the components and raw materials for these products?' 'What unique products or features does this target market require?' While these questions are being asked today by senior managers of many large corporations as part of their global strategy, they will be asked more frequently and at lower levels of the organization as part of their operational strategy.

Where will these 'good' people come from? They need to be trained for tomorrow's needs, which many of our government training schemes, universities and colleges are not yet fully addressing. For the moment, you may have to train them yourself. Several corporations have developed their own 'universities' to educate their people in what is needed for success in the future. Smaller companies are banding together, sometimes with a local college or university, to ensure their people are taught the needed skills. The key message here is not to wait. In the long run, the only thing that differentiates you from the competition is your people. Make sure yours are in the lead.

Competing with the best in the world, everywhere in the world

As mentioned earlier, the export of manufactured goods is probably at its peak right now. It will soon start to diminish and be replaced by the export of factories into or close to every target market. I believe this trend has already started but is not yet in full swing. These factories will be small, responsive and customer focused. They will be part of a large corporation but will operate autonomously. They may also be part of a virtual corporation.

A company, then, that wants to participate in a given market will site a factory in or close to the market-place. Competitors who also want a share of this market will also have factories close to or in the target market. Instead of competing 5000 miles apart, today's scenario, competition will be 50 miles apart. What will spell success or disaster in this brave new world?

It is obvious you won't be successful, factory against factory. The days when you could be successful as an individual company are long gone. The

Spirit of Saint Louis, Charles Lindbergh's plane, and his successful solo flight across the Atlantic was a triumph of individualism. The Concorde is a triumph of teamwork, not only in the building of the plane but also in its successful regular schedule shuttling back and forth across the Atlantic. Tomorrow's battle will be supply chain against supply chain, virtual corporation against virtual corporation, value chain against value chain, and groups of companies against groups of companies. If your team of companies is faster than the competition, you'll get the order. If you have better technology, you'll get the order. If you are less expensive, you'll get the order. If you give better service, you'll get the order. As an individual company your job will be to do your piece of the total well. Your success will depend on *all* the pieces being done well.

The challenge, of course, is that a competitor can show up in one of your established markets with new technology, better people, a better network of companies for support and a better management style and steal huge chunks of your business before you can respond. Staying at the forefront of all these issues will be the only way to stay successful.

New competitors will be evolving constantly and the changes coming will lower many current barriers to entry. Even automobiles, conceptually safe today from new competitors, will find companies starting up to produce small numbers of cars for a limited niche market or small geographic area. The traditional, enormous capital to do this will no longer be required with modular designs and many first tier suppliers looking for business.

These new competitors will be a real threat to existing companies because they will have no existing investments to defend. If they can address the specific needs of a target market better, they will quickly become a factor to contend with.

What should a company do?

Today's competitive edge comes from profitably delighting customers. I don't see this changing for at least the next 50 years. The way to do this will change over the next 50 years. Earlier chapters of this book explained how to profitably delight customers today. Make sure you implement all these ideas quickly to squeeze maximum value out of today's ideas.

Start thinking about tomorrow. Firstly, consider the global market-place and decide where you would like to sell. Evaluate your product, its needed speed of response, its degree of uniqueness or customization to customer needs, its value density and so on to determine when you should build close to or in your target marketplaces. This doesn't necessarily mean in your own facility, it could just as easily mean in a third party subcontractor.

Secondly, start broadening your view of your support companies. Do you have good partnerships today? Can you develop them further? Are there other companies out there you should work with to gain some advantage you cannot get yourself? This should slowly evolve into a virtual corporation.

Thirdly, start everyone thinking about agility. What does it mean for your company? No one knows for sure all the elements of agility and what it truly means. Make sure you don't think it is a simple extension of JIT and TQM, it isn't. It has far more reaching implications than this. Think again about the changes needed for the three-day car to be a viable proposition.

Fourthly, become a leader in technology, especially of communication. Moving information long distances is very inexpensive and will partially replace moving products long distances. As an example, the Irish government has an extensive training program to develop its people to be excellent software writers. It realizes, being on the western edge of the European Common Market, that it is too far away from the primary markets to be much of an exporter of products. But, at almost no charge, it can export software electronically to anywhere in the world earning it the hard currency it desperately needs. You will need excellent communications and other technology to function well in the global virtual corporation.

Fifthly, educate and train your people to be excellent in tomorrow's competitive world. Broaden their knowledge about the business in total and about the global market-place. Especially develop their people skills in teamwork, diversity consciousness and languages. These will all be needed in the global, agile, virtual corporation. Lastly, stay customer focused. I don't mean so you delight customers, that is *not* the objective, but so you delight them *profitably*. Be selective about who you delight and what you delight them with. The results will speak for themselves.

Bibliography

Agile Product Development for Mass Customization, David Anderson, Irwin, 1997.

Cycle Time Reduction, Jerry Harbour, Quality Resources, 1996.

Orchestrating Success, Richard Ling and Walter Goddard, Oliver Wight Publications, 1988.

The Team Net Factor, Jessica Lipsack and Jeffrey Stamps, Oliver Wight Publications, 1993.

Competitive Manufacturing, 2nd edition, Hal Mather, Woodhead Publishing, 1998.

'Extend Profits, Not Product Lines', John Quelch and David Kenny, *Harvard Business Review*, Sept/Oct 1994.

A Revolution in Manufacturing – The SMED System, Shigeo Shingo, Productivity Press, 1985.

Developing Products in Half the Time, Preston Smith and Donald Reinertsen, Van Nostrand Reinhold, 1991.

Index